# THE NINE RACES
## THE FORGOTTEN ORIGIN OF HUMANITY

## MICHAEL VINCENT

First Edition, 2026

ISBN: 978-1-971762-86-9

# CONTENTS

# INTRODUCTION

This book presents an account of human origins in which ancient populations possessed genuinely distinct biological capabilities, actual genetic variations that made some groups more intelligent, more organizationally capable, and more innovative than others.

The narrative describes races that were biologically distinct from other races, populations that were less able or more endowed by nature, and the effects of superior peoples migrating and mixing with primitive populations. It presents an explicit hierarchy of human capability rooted in ancestry and genetics extending back hundreds of thousands of years.

These claims may appear to mirror discredited racial perspectives from the 19th and 20th centuries. The language may resemble thinking that justified destructive practices like colonialism and slavery.

One distinction must be stated at the outset: biological capability and human worth are entirely separate categories. Every individual possesses equal value regardless of which ancient populations contributed to their ancestry. Nothing in this account changes that.

This account differs from historical racial pseudoscience in crucial ways. The races described here existed hundreds of thousands of years ago and disappeared through interbreeding tens of thousands of years before recorded history began. By the time recognizable civilizations emerged—Sumer, Egypt, China—racial blending had transformed the nine original races into the diverse populations of recorded history.

Every modern human carries ancestry from multiple ancient sources. Contemporary racial categories do not map onto the nine origins described here. Modern populations are complex mixtures that combine different ancestral streams in different proportions, modified by thirty millennia of additional development, migration, and blending. The ancient populations no longer exist in pure form.

This material derives from an unusual source that presents itself as authoritative information about planetary history. The racial narrative was adapted from this source while remaining faithful to its essential claims.

Reports about actual historical differences between ancient populations operate in a different category than ideologies invented to justify oppression. The former represents observation; the latter represents rationalization. Whether the source merits credibility remains for each reader to determine.

The past demonstrated the cost of racial thinking in lives, in suffering, in civilizational damage. Any suggestion that populations differ in native capability sounds like backsliding toward discredited ideas. The morally clean position insists that all human variation is cultural and environmental—that genetic differences between populations are trivial and meaningless.

The account presented here requires holding two truths: biological differences between populations were real in the past and remain real today, though in heavily blended form. Spiritual equality—the worth of every individual soul—was absolute then and remains absolute now. Ancient populations differed in capability. Modern people carry mixed ancestry from many sources. Individual human value transcends all biological variation.

Language has been chosen carefully throughout this text to describe biological history accurately while avoiding unnecessarily offensive terminology. Where the source material uses terms now considered outdated, alternative phrasing captures the intended meaning without perpetuating potentially harmful rhetoric. Some challenging language may remain where modification would obscure the actual claims being presented.

Readers will encounter descriptions that resemble racial hierarchy. Each instance describes ancient populations that no longer exist as distinct groups. This framework describes deep history without justifying modern racism. No account of the past, however factual, can justify prejudice, discrimination, or claims of superiority among people living today.

Understanding where humans originated, with complex mixed ancestry from nine different sources, provides context for comprehending both remarkable diversity and fundamental unity. The biological realities were ancient populations that disappeared through the mixing that created us.

This book tells that story.

# 1

# BEFORE THERE WERE RACES

Before there were races, before there were humans, there was a million-year journey of evolutionary development that prepared the way for the emergence of true human beings on planet Earth.

This is not the story of random chance. The appearance of humanity represented the culmination of potentials built into the original life processes nearly 600 million years ago and developed through successive stages of increasingly complex organisms. The process was evolutionary—involving natural selection, environmental adaptation, and biological variation—but the capacity for eventual human emergence was built into the system from the beginning.

The story begins with lemurs.

## The Early Lemur Types

Slightly over one million years ago, the immediate ancestors of humankind made their appearance through three successive and sudden mutations stemming from early stock of the lemur type of placental mammal. The early lemurs that would spawn humanity bore no direct relation to the gibbons and apes already living in Eurasia and northern Africa. Nor were they offspring of the modern lemur type, though all shared a common ancestor long since extinct.

The dominant genetic factors of these early lemurs were derived from the western or American group of evolving life forms. But before establishing the direct line of human ancestry, this strain was reinforced by contributions from the central life development that had evolved in Africa. The eastern life group contributed little to the actual production of the human species.

Several million years ago, the North American type lemurs had migrated westward over the Bering land bridge and slowly made their way southwestward along the Asiatic coast. These migrating populations finally reached the region lying between the then-expanded Mediterranean Sea and the elevating mountainous regions of the Indian peninsula. In these lands to the west of India, they united with other favorable strains, thus establishing the ancestry of the human race.

With the passing of time, the seacoast of India southwest of the mountains gradually submerged, completely isolating the life of this region. There was no avenue of approach to, or escape from, this Mesopotamian or Persian peninsula except to the north, and that passage was repeatedly cut off by southern glacial invasions. It was in this then almost paradisiacal area, and from the most capable descendants of this lemur type of mammal, that there sprang two great groups: the simian tribes of modern times and the present-day human species.

## The Dawn Mammals

The Mesopotamian dawn mammals, the direct descendants of the North American lemur type of placental mammal, suddenly appeared. They represented a genuine leap forward in the evolutionary process.

Active, intelligent, nearly three feet tall—the dawn mammals marked a genuine evolutionary leap. Though they didn't habitually walk upright, they could stand erect when needed. Hairy, agile, chattering like monkeys, they differed from simian tribes in one crucial respect: they ate meat. They possessed a primitive opposable thumb as well as a highly useful grasping big toe. From this point onward, the prehuman species would successively develop the opposable thumb while progressively losing the grasping power of the great toe. The later ape tribes retained the grasping big toe but never developed the human type of thumb.

These dawn mammals attained full growth when three or four years of age and had a potential life span of about twenty years on average. Offspring were usually born singly, though twins were occasional.

The members of this new species had the largest brains for their size of any animal that had theretofore existed on Earth. They experienced many of the emotions and shared numerous instincts that would later characterize primitive humans. They were highly curious and exhibited considerable elation when successful at any undertaking. Food hunger and sexual drive were well developed, and definite mate selection manifested itself in a crude form of courtship and choice of partners. They would fight fiercely in defense of their kindred and were quite tender in family associations, possessing a sense of self-abasement bordering on shame and remorse. They were very affectionate and touchingly loyal to their mates, but if circumstances separated them, they would choose new partners.

Being small of stature and having keen minds to realize the dangers of their forest habitat, they developed an extraordinary fear response that led to wise precautionary measures contributing enormously to their survival. They constructed crude shelters in high treetops, which eliminated many of the perils of ground life. The beginning of humanity's fear tendencies dates specifically from these days.

These dawn mammals developed more of a tribal spirit than had ever been previously exhibited. They were highly gregarious but nevertheless exceedingly pugnacious when disturbed in the ordinary pursuit of their routine life. They displayed fiery tempers when their anger was fully aroused. However, their bellicose natures served a constructive purpose: dominant groups did not hesitate to make war on their neighbors, and through selective survival, the species progressively improved. They soon dominated the life of smaller creatures in their region, and very few of the older non-carnivorous monkeylike tribes survived their expansion.

These aggressive creatures multiplied and spread over the Mesopotamian peninsula for more than one thousand years, constantly improving in physical type and general intelligence. It was just seventy generations after this new tribe had taken origin from the highest type of lemur ancestor that the next epoch-making development occurred: the sudden differentiation of the ancestors of the next vital step in the evolution of human beings on Earth.

## The Mid-Mammals

Early in the career of the dawn mammals, in the treetop abode of an exceptional pair of these agile creatures, twins were born—one male and one female. Compared with their ancestors, they were handsome creatures. They had little hair on their bodies, but this was no disability as they lived in a warm and equable climate.

These twins grew to be a little over four feet in height—considerably larger than their parents. They had longer legs and shorter arms than their forebears. They possessed almost perfectly opposable thumbs, just about as well adapted for diversified work as the present human thumb. They walked upright, having feet almost as well suited for walking as those of the later human races.

Their brains were smaller than those of human beings, but comparatively much larger than those of their ancestors. The twins early displayed exceptional intelligence and were soon recognized as the heads of the whole tribe of dawn mammals, instituting a primitive form of social organization and a crude economic division of labor. This brother and sister mated and soon enjoyed the society of twenty-one children much like themselves—all more than four feet tall and in every way superior to the ancestral species. This new group formed the nucleus of the mid-mammals.

When the numbers of this new group grew large, war—relentless war—broke out between them and their dawn mammal ancestors. When the terrible struggle was over, not a single individual of the pre-existent ancestral race remained alive. The less numerous but more powerful and intelligent offshoot of the species had survived at the expense of their ancestors.

For almost fifteen thousand years—six hundred generations—this creature became the terror of that part of the world. All of the great and vicious animals of former times had perished. The large beasts native to these regions were not carnivorous, and the larger species of the cat family—lions and tigers—had not yet invaded this peculiarly sheltered area of Earth's surface. Therefore, these mid-mammals grew valiant and subdued their entire corner of creation.

Compared with the ancestral species, the mid-mammals were an improvement in every way. Even their potential life span was longer, being about twenty-five years. A number of rudimentary human traits appeared in this new species. In addition to the innate propensities exhibited by their ancestors, these mid-mammals were capable of showing disgust in certain repulsive situations. They possessed a well-defined hoarding instinct, hiding food for subsequent use and being greatly given to the collection of smooth round pebbles and certain types of round stones suitable for defensive and offensive ammunition.

These mid-mammals were the first to exhibit definite construction propensity, as shown in their rivalry in the building of both treetop homes and their many-tunneled subterranean retreats. They were the first species of mammals ever to provide for safety in both arboreal and underground shelters. They largely forsook the trees as places of abode, living on the ground during the day and sleeping in the treetops at night.

As time passed, natural increase in numbers eventually resulted in serious food competition and sexual rivalry, culminating in a series of internecine battles that nearly destroyed the entire species. These struggles continued until only one group of less than one hundred individuals remained alive. But peace once more prevailed, and this lone surviving tribe built anew its treetop bedrooms and once again resumed a normal and semipeaceful existence.

The evolutionary process hung by the narrowest of threads. Had certain chance events occurred differently at critical moments, the whole course of evolution would have been markedly changed. The immediate lemurlike ancestor of the dawn-mammal species escaped death no less than five times by mere hairbreadth margins. But the closest call of all came when lightning struck the tree in which the prospective mother of the twins was sleeping.

## The Primate Twins

Both of these mid-mammal parents were severely shocked and badly burned by the lightning strike. Three of their seven children were killed by this bolt from the skies. These evolving animals were almost superstitious about such events. This couple, whose treetop home had been struck, were actually the leaders of the more progressive group of the mid-mammal species. Following their example and driven by fear, more than half the tribe—embracing the more intelligent families—moved about two miles away from this locality and began the construction of new treetop abodes and new ground shelters for use in times of sudden danger.

Soon after the completion of their home, this couple—veterans of so many struggles—found themselves the proud parents of twins. These were the most interesting and important animals ever to have been born into the world up to that time, for they were the first of the new species of Primates constituting the next vital step in prehuman evolution.

Around the same time as the birth of these Primate twins, another couple—a peculiarly underdeveloped male and female of the mid-mammal tribe, both mentally and physically inferior—also gave birth to twins. These twins, one male and one female, were indifferent to conquest and concerned only with obtaining food. Since they would not eat flesh, they soon lost all interest in seeking prey. These less capable twins became the founders of the modern simian tribes. Their descendants sought the warmer southern regions with mild climates and an abundance of tropical fruits, where they have continued much as of that day except for those branches that mated with the earlier types of gibbons and apes and have greatly deteriorated in consequence.

Thus it may be readily seen that humans and apes are related only in that they sprang from the mid-mammals, a tribe in which there occurred the contemporaneous birth and subsequent segregation of two pairs of twins: the inferior pair destined to produce the modern types of monkey, baboon, chimpanzee, and gorilla; the superior pair destined to continue the line of ascent that evolved into humanity itself.

Modern humans and the simians sprang from the same tribe and species but not from the same parents. Human ancestors descended from the superior strains of the selected remnant of this mid-mammal tribe, whereas the modern simians (excepting certain pre-existent types of lemurs, gibbons, apes, and other monkeylike creatures) are the descendants of the most inferior couple of this mid-mammal group—a couple who survived only by hiding themselves in a subterranean food-storage retreat for more than two weeks during the last fierce battle of their tribe, emerging only after the hostilities were well over.

## The Primates

The superior Primate twins were of an unusual order. They had still less hair on their bodies than their parents and, when very young, insisted on walking upright. Their ancestors had always learned to walk on their hind legs, but these twins stood erect from the beginning. They attained a height of over five feet, and their heads grew larger in comparison with others among the tribe. While early learning to communicate with each other by means of signs and sounds, they were never able to make their fellows understand these new symbols.

By the time they were fourteen, the twins had left the tribe entirely, heading west to raise a family and found what would become the Primate species.

The Primates came to occupy a region on the west coast of the Mesopotamian peninsula as it then projected into the southern sea, while the less intelligent and closely related tribes lived around the peninsula point and up the eastern shore line.

They were more human and less animal than their mid-mammal predecessors. The skeletal proportions of this new species were very similar to those of the primitive human races. The human type of hand and foot had fully developed, and these creatures could walk and even run as well as any of their later-day human descendants. They largely abandoned tree life, though continuing to resort to the treetops as a safety measure at night, for like their earlier ancestors, they were greatly subject to fear. The increased use of their hands did much to develop inherent brain power, but they did not yet possess minds that could really be called human.

Although in emotional nature the Primates differed little from their forebears, they exhibited more of a human trend in all of their propensities. They were splendid and superior animals, reaching maturity at about ten years of age and having a natural life span of about forty years—had they been able to die natural deaths. But in those early days very few animals ever died naturally; the struggle for existence was altogether too intense.

## The Last Link

For almost nine hundred generations of development, covering about twenty-one thousand years from the origin of the dawn mammals, this species continued to evolve. And then, suddenly, something extraordinary occurred.

Two remarkable creatures were born, the first true human beings.

Thus it was that the dawn mammals, springing from the North American lemur type, gave origin to the mid-mammals, and these mid-mammals in turn produced advanced species, who became the immediate ancestors of the primitive human race. These tribes were the last vital link in the evolution of humanity, but in less than five thousand years not a single individual of these extraordinary tribes would remain alive.

The stage was set for the appearance of the first beings who would possess genuine moral capacity, spiritual awareness, and true free will. The long ascent through lemurs, dawn mammals, mid-mammals, and primates had reached its culmination.

On a specific day approximately 993,511 years ago, something unprecedented happened in the history of planet Earth. Two children were born who were qualitatively different from every creature that had come before them.

They were human.[1]

# 2

# THE FIRST HUMANS

Nearly one million years ago, two exceptional children were born to primate parents who, despite their own considerable advancement over their mid-mammal ancestors, could not have fully comprehended what their offspring represented.

In many respects, these twins—one male and one female—would prove to be the most significant pair of human beings that have ever lived on Earth. They were the actual parents of all humankind, superior in every way to many of their immediate descendants, and radically different from all of their ancestors, both immediate and remote. For clarity in this account, we will refer to the male twin as Andon and the female twin as Fonta—names that signify their role as the first father and first mother of humanity. Throughout their lives, they called each other by different names: Sonta-an (meaning "loved by mother") and Sonta-en (meaning "loved by father"). They gave themselves these names, and the meanings reveal their mutual regard and affection. The parents of this first human couple were apparently little different from the average of their primate tribe, though they were among its more intelligent members—that group which had first learned to throw stones and to use clubs in fighting. They also made use of sharp spicules of stone, flint, and bone.

These two children possessed perfect human thumbs, as had many of their ancestors, while they had just as perfect feet as present-day human races. They were walkers and runners, not climbers. The grasping function of the big toe was absent—completely absent. When danger drove them to the treetops, they climbed just like humans of today would, ascending the trunk of a tree like a bear rather than swinging up by the branches as would a chimpanzee or gorilla.

These first human beings (and their descendants) reached full maturity at twelve years of age and possessed a potential life span of about seventy-five years. The advance they represented over their parents was not primarily physical—though their bodies were superior in proportion and capability—but mental and spiritual. Many new emotions appeared early in these human twins. They experienced admiration for both objects and other beings and exhibited considerable vanity. But the most profound advance in emotional development was the sudden appearance of worshipful feelings: awe, reverence, humility, and even a primitive form of gratitude. Fear, joined with ignorance of natural phenomena, was about to give birth to primitive religion.

Not only were such human feelings manifested, but many more highly evolved sentiments were also present in rudimentary form. They were mildly cognizant of pity, shame, and reproach and were acutely conscious of love, hate, and revenge, being also susceptible to marked feelings of jealousy.

What made these two different from every creature that had come before them? It was the appearance of will—the capacity for genuine moral choice, for worshipful awareness, and for abstract thought. These were not merely more intelligent animals. They were beings capable of choosing to do what they believed to be right even when it contradicted their immediate desires. They could conceive of something beyond themselves. They could imagine futures that did not yet exist and then work deliberately to bring those futures into being. They were, in the truest sense, human.

## The Momentous Decision

These first two humans were a considerable trial to their primate parents. They were extraordinarily curious and adventurous, nearly losing their lives on numerous occasions before they were eight years old. As it was, they were well scarred by the time they reached twelve years of age.

The decision of Andon and Fonta to flee from the primate tribes implies a quality of mind far above the baser intelligence that characterized so many of their later descendants who stooped to mate with their cousins of the simian tribes. Their vague feeling of being something more than mere animals was due to the possession of personality and was augmented by an inner spiritual awareness that transcended anything their ancestors had experienced.

When the twins were about nine years old, they journeyed down the river one bright day and held a momentous conference. On this eventful day, they arrived at an understanding to live with and for each other. This was the first of a series of such agreements which finally culminated in the decision to flee from their inferior animal associates and to journey northward, little knowing that they were thus to found the human race.

Shortly before their departure from the home forests, tragedy struck. The twins lost their mother in a gibbon raid. While she did not possess their intelligence, she did have a worthy mammalian affection of a high order for her offspring, and she fearlessly gave her life in the attempt to save the wonderful pair. Her sacrifice was not in vain, for she held off the enemy until the father arrived with reinforcements and put the invaders to rout.

Soon after this young couple forsook their associates to found the human race, their primate father became disconsolate— heartbroken. He refused to eat, even when food was brought to him by his other children. His brilliant offspring having been lost, life did not seem worth living among his ordinary fellows. He wandered off into the forest, was set upon by hostile gibbons, and was beaten to death.

## The Northern Flight

After Andon and Fonta had decided to flee northward, they succumbed to their fears for a time—especially the fear of displeasing their father and immediate family (though this fear came before his death). They envisaged being set upon by hostile relatives and thus recognized the possibility of meeting death at the hands of their already jealous tribesmen.

As youngsters, the twins had spent most of their time in each other's company and for this reason had never been overly popular with their animal cousins of the tribe. Nor had they improved their standing by building a separate and very superior tree home.

It was in this new home among the treetops, one night after they had been awakened by a violent storm, that—as they held each other in fearful and fond embrace—they finally and fully made up their minds to flee from the tribal habitat and the home treetops.

They had already prepared a crude treetop retreat some half-day's journey to the north. This was their secret and safe hiding place for the first day away from the home forests. Notwithstanding that the twins shared the primates' deathly fear of being on the ground at nighttime, they set forth shortly before nightfall on their northern trek. While it required unusual courage for them to undertake this night journey even with a full moon, they correctly concluded that they were less likely to be missed and pursued by their tribesmen and relatives. They safely made their previously prepared rendezvous shortly after midnight.

## The Discovery of Fire

On their northward journey, they discovered an exposed flint deposit and, finding many stones suitably shaped for various uses, gathered up a supply for the future. In attempting to chip these flints so that they would be better adapted for certain purposes, Andon discovered their sparking quality and conceived the idea of building fire. But the notion did not take firm hold of him at the time, as the climate was still salubrious and there was little need of fire.

But the autumn sun was getting lower in the sky, and as they journeyed northward, the nights grew cooler and cooler. They had already been forced to make use of animal skins for warmth. Before they had been away from home one moon, Andon signified to his mate that he thought he could make fire with the flint. They tried for two months to utilize the flint spark for kindling a fire but met only with failure. Each day this couple would strike the flints and endeavor to ignite wood.

Finally, one evening about the time of the setting sun, the secret of the technique was unraveled when it occurred to Fonta to climb a nearby tree to secure an abandoned bird's nest. The nest was dry and highly inflammable and consequently flared right up into a full blaze the moment the spark fell upon it. They were so surprised and startled at their success that they almost lost the fire, but they saved it by the addition of suitable fuel. Then began the first search for firewood by the parents of all humankind.

This was one of the most joyous moments in their short but eventful lives. All night long they sat up watching their fire burn, vaguely realizing that they had made a discovery that would make it possible for them to defy climate and thus forever to be independent of their animal relatives of the southern lands. After three days' rest and enjoyment of the fire, they journeyed on.

The primate ancestors of Andon had often replenished fire that had been kindled by lightning, but never before had the creatures of Earth possessed a method of starting fire at will. It would be a long time, however, before the twins learned that dry moss and other materials would kindle fire just as well as birds' nests.

## The First Family

Almost two years passed between the night of the twins' flight and the birth of their first child. They named him Sontad, and he holds a quiet distinction in planetary history: he was the first creature born on this world who was wrapped in protective coverings at the time of birth. The detail seems small, but it marks a threshold. The animal world does not swaddle its young. Something new had appeared—an instinct to care for increasingly helpless infants that would characterize the development of intellectual mind as contrasted with the purely animal type. Human babies are born more vulnerable than almost any other mammalian offspring, and that vulnerability is the price of a larger brain and a longer childhood. The extended dependency that followed would create the opening for something no other species had achieved: the deliberate passing of knowledge from one generation to the next.

Andon and Fonta had nineteen children in all. In an environment of predators, harsh climate, disease, and accident, raising nineteen children to any age represents a remarkable achievement—a testament to the practical intelligence that distinguished this couple from everything that had come before them. Within their lifetimes, they enjoyed the company of almost fifty grandchildren and half a dozen great-grandchildren. From two individuals to a community of multiple generations in a single lifespan: the human race was not merely surviving, it was expanding.

The family was domiciled in four adjoining rock shelters, or semicaves, three of which were interconnected by hallways excavated in the soft limestone with flint tools devised by Andon's children. This last detail deserves emphasis. It was the children, not Andon himself, who designed the specialized tools and carved passages through solid rock to connect the family's living spaces. The second generation was already innovating beyond the first. Whatever Andon and Fonta had kindled in their offspring—through teaching, through example, through the sheer pressure of survival—it was producing minds capable of original engineering. A tool-creating intelligence was now functioning in conjunction with an implement-using hand, and the results were literally reshaping the landscape.

## The Clan

These early Andonites evinced a very marked clannish spirit. They hunted in groups and never strayed far from the homesite. They seemed to realize, on some deep level, that they were an isolated and unique group of living beings and should therefore avoid becoming separated. This was not mere animal herding instinct—it was something closer to collective identity, a sense of us that bound them together more tightly than biological kinship alone could explain.

The children formed partnerships among themselves—there being no other option—and the clan grew inward, intensifying its bonds with each generation. Sontad married his eldest sister, and the pattern of close intermarriage continued out of necessity. The isolation that protected the clan's unique qualities also constrained its genetic options. But for now, the strategy worked: the family held, the population grew, and the Andonite way of life consolidated around a shared homesite, a shared language, and shared techniques passed from parent to child.

Andon had invented the first hafted weapon while still living among the Primates—a sharp piece of flint fastened to the end of a club with animal tendons. It was a crude device, but he used it on no fewer than a dozen occasions to save his own life and Fonta's. During their northward journey, he discovered an exposed flint deposit, and finding many stones suitably shaped for various uses, he gathered a supply for the future. In attempting to chip these flints for specific purposes, he discovered their sparking quality—the breakthrough that would eventually lead to the mastery of fire.

His descendants built rapidly on these foundations. They discovered the throwing stick and the harpoon. They became highly skillful in the fashioning of flint tools, traveling far and wide in search of quality stone—much as later peoples would journey to the ends of the earth in quest of gold, platinum, and diamonds. The Andonites were fearless and successful hunters who, with the exception of wild berries and certain tree fruits, lived exclusively on flesh.

## Language and Tragedy

Language developed alongside technology, each driving the other forward. Before their departure from the Primates tribe, Andon and Fonta had already worked out an improved sign and word language of almost fifty ideas—a modest vocabulary by any later standard, but an enormous leap beyond the crude communicative techniques of their ancestors. They tried to teach these new signs and symbols to their parents, but with only limited success. The gap between the first humans and their animal forebears was already too wide to bridge through instruction alone.

In the generations that followed, this initial vocabulary expanded continuously. Before the great dispersion of the Andonic clans, a well-developed language had evolved, growing almost daily as these active, restless, and curious people coined new words for new inventions and new environmental adaptations. This tongue became the common speech of the early human family and persisted until the much later appearance of the colored races introduced entirely new linguistic traditions.

Andon and Fonta labored incessantly for the nurture and uplift of their clan. They lived to the age of forty-two—a full lifespan for their era, when few creatures died of old age and most succumbed to accident, predation, or disease. Their deaths, when they came, were sudden and devastating. During an earthquake, an overhanging rock collapsed onto the shelter where several family members had gathered. Andon and Fonta were killed instantly, along with five of their children and eleven grandchildren. Almost twenty more descendants suffered serious injuries.

Upon the death of his parents, Sontad—despite a seriously injured foot from the same disaster—immediately assumed leadership of the clan, ably assisted by his wife, his eldest sister. Their first act was to roll up stones to entomb their dead: parents, brothers, sisters, children. It was not theology that drove them to it. Their ideas about survival after death were vague and indefinite, largely shaped by their fantastic and varied dream life. But something compelled them to mark the passing of the dead with deliberate, physical ceremony—to distinguish the death of a person from the death of an animal. This impulse, arising before any doctrine or creed, may be the oldest recognizably human behavior: the refusal to let death pass without acknowledgment.

## Legacy

The family held together for twenty generations after Andon and Fonta's death, with leadership passing through an unbroken line of Sontad's descendants. That continuity—maintained without writing, without law, without any formal institution—speaks to the strength of the bonds these first humans forged through shared language, shared memory, and shared identity.

In many respects, Andon and Fonta were the most remarkable pair of human beings that have ever lived. They were in every way superior to many of their immediate descendants, and they were radically different from all of their ancestors. They did not merely survive; they created the conditions under which survival could become something more. They proved that two individuals, armed with nothing but courage, intelligence, and each other, could walk away from everything they knew and build the foundation of a species.

Theirs is the most heroic and fascinating chapter in all the history of this world: the story of the evolution, life struggles, death, and legacy of the unique parents of all mankind.[1]

# 3
# THE PEOPLE OF THE DAWN

For twenty generations, the family of Andon and Fonta held together. That is a significant span of social continuity—roughly five hundred years of unbroken kinship, shared language, and collective identity, all without writing, without permanent architecture, without any of the institutional scaffolding that later civilizations would depend on. The glue was simpler: blood, proximity, and the shared awareness that they were something new in the world and should not allow themselves to be scattered.

But no family can hold together forever, and the forces that eventually broke the Andonites apart were as old as life itself: too many mouths for too little food, and the friction that inevitably builds when growing numbers of proud, aggressive people share limited space. The twentieth generation marked the beginning of dispersion—not a single dramatic exodus, but a slow unraveling, as family lines drifted apart and established their own territories.

## The Andonite Nature

Before tracing that dispersion, it is worth pausing over what kind of people the Andonites were.

Their social organization developed quickly. The tribal patterns of their animal ancestors had already foreshadowed the beginnings of social convention, and the Andonites—with their enhanced emotions and greater mental capacity—immediately elaborated these into a genuine division of labor within the clan. They were exceedingly imitative. But the play instinct was only slightly developed, and the sense of humor was almost entirely absent. Primitive man smiled occasionally but never laughed heartily. Humor would be the contribution of a much later race.

They were not sensitive to pain the way later humans would be. Childbirth was not a painful ordeal for Fonta or her immediate descendants. They were hardy, practical, and physically tough—well-suited to the demanding environment that shaped them.

In appearance, they had black eyes and a swarthy complexion, something between yellow and red. Of all living peoples, they most closely resembled the modern Inuit. They were the first creatures to wear animal skins against the cold, and they carried little more body hair than humans do today.

Their virtues were fierce and immediate. The males fought heroically for their mates and children. The females were devoted mothers. They possessed a touching affection for their comrades and a real, if crude, idea of friendship. In battle, a warrior would fight with one hand while using the other to drag an injured companion to safety. Many of the noblest traits of later humanity were foreshadowed—touchingly, if imperfectly—in these primitive people.

But their limitations were equally stark. Their loyalty extended no further than the immediate clan. They would die without hesitation to protect their children, yet they could not conceive of trying to make the world better for their grandchildren. Altruism in the broader sense had not yet been born. And the two things that dominated their mental life were hunting and vengeance—obtaining food and settling scores with neighboring groups.

This combination of fierce loyalty and fierce aggression proved catastrophic as the population grew. Family feuds escalated into tribal wars. The losses fell disproportionately on the best and brightest—the bold, the skilled, the innovative—because these were the ones who led in battle. Some of the most valuable strains of ability and intelligence were forever lost to the world. The early race and its primitive civilization were genuinely threatened with extinction by their own incessant warfare.

The hard truth, applicable far beyond the Andonites, is that it is impossible to induce primitive beings to live together in peace for long. Man is the descendant of fighting animals, and when closely associated, uncultured people irritate and offend each other.

The language that Andon and Fonta had begun—and that their descendants expanded daily across twenty generations—survived the warfare and would outlast the Andonites themselves.

Leadership, too, showed remarkable continuity. The original Andonic clan maintained an unbroken line of rulers descended from Sontad until the twenty-seventh generation—when, for the first time, no male heir appeared among Sontad's direct descendants, and two rival claimants plunged the clan into a war for supremacy.

## Into Ice

The geography of those times gave the Andonites few options. To the east lay the arid Tibetan highlands, thirty thousand feet above sea level. To the south and west, the expanded Mediterranean Sea stretched eastward to the Indian Ocean. Only the north was open—and so northward they went, farther and farther, until they met the slowly advancing wall of the third great glacier.

Before the ice sheet reached France and the British Isles, the descendants of Andon and Fonta had pushed westward across Europe and established more than a thousand separate settlements along the great rivers leading to the then-warm waters of the North Sea. The Somme valley in France became a particular stronghold. The Somme was the one river the glaciers never altered—it ran to the sea then as it does now—and the Andonites lived along its banks for tens of thousands of years. This is why so much archaeological evidence of early human habitation clusters along this river valley.

These were not tree dwellers, though in emergencies they still scrambled into the branches. They were not true cave dwellers either, though later ice advances would eventually push their descendants underground. The Andonites preferred a middle ground: overhanging cliffs along rivers and hillside grottoes that offered both shelter from the weather and a clear view of approaching threats. They could enjoy the warmth of their fires in these settings without choking on smoke—a practical advantage that shaped their settlement patterns for millennia.

They also showed surprising ingenuity in construction. They became remarkably clever at disguising their sheltered camps, and they developed a distinctive form of architecture: dome-shaped stone huts, small enough to crawl into, sealed at night by rolling a large stone across the entrance—a stone placed inside during construction, before the roof was completed, for exactly this purpose. These were not grand structures, but they represent genuine engineering: a problem foreseen and solved during the building process, not after.

By 950,000 years ago—roughly fifty thousand years after Andon and Fonta's time—their descendants had spread from England in the west to Java in the east, and eventually as far as Tasmania. The western migrants fared better, maintaining more of their ancestors' capabilities. The eastern groups mingled more readily with less-developed populations, and the resulting mixed offspring gradually diluted the Andonic heritage. When these mixed descendants later migrated back northward and interbred with the purer Andonic stock, the effect was consistently degrading. The early dawn civilization was slowly being undermined from within.

## Onagar and the Breath Giver

As the Andonites scattered and their cultural continuity frayed, they entered a long decline. For nearly ten thousand years after the great dispersion began, the spiritual and cultural status of the clans retrogressed steadily.

Then came Onagar.

Born 983,323 years before the twentieth century, Onagar assumed leadership of the scattered tribes, brought peace among them, and accomplished something no one before him had managed: he united them in the worship of a single deity, whom he called the "Breath Giver to men and animals." The prayer he taught his people reveals both their priorities and their emerging spiritual awareness:

*O Breath of Life, give us this day our daily food, deliver us from the curse of the ice, save us from our forest enemies, and with mercy receive us into the Great Beyond.*

Every phrase addresses a concrete reality of Andonite life—hunger, cold, predators—yet the prayer reaches beyond the material toward something Onagar called the Great Beyond. This was not a sophisticated theology. But it was genuine religion: an acknowledgment that human life pointed toward something larger than survival.

Onagar established his headquarters at a settlement called Oban, on the northern shores of the ancient Mediterranean near what is now the Caspian Sea. From Oban he sent teachers to the remote settlements—the world's first missionaries. These emissaries carried Onagar's doctrines of one Deity and the Great Beyond to scattered Andonite communities across the known world. They also introduced a practical innovation: they were the first human beings to cook meat, the first to regularly use fire in food preparation. They roasted flesh on sticks, on hot stones, and eventually over open flame.

Onagar lived to sixty-nine and instituted an efficient tribal government that would not be equaled for millennia. He organized primitive peoples into a real society. Under his leadership, these simple people possessed a real, though primitive, religion.

But it did not last. After Onagar's death, his achievements eroded. His descendants lost what he had built. By 900,000 years ago, the arts of Andon and Fonta and the culture of Onagar were vanishing from the face of the earth. Culture, religion, and even basic flintworking had sunk to their lowest ebb.

This is the central pattern of the Andonite period, and perhaps the most sobering lesson of early human history: biological capacity alone cannot sustain civilization. The Andonites manifested a degree of intelligence that their retrogressing descendants would not match for half a million years. Yet without the cultural infrastructure to preserve and transmit their achievements—without writing, without institutions, without any mechanism more durable than living memory— each generation's gains remained perpetually vulnerable to the next generation's losses. What one great leader built, the absence of the next great leader could undo.

The Andonites proved that humans could think, create, worship, and organize. They had not yet proven that humans could hold onto these achievements across time. That challenge would require something the Andonites alone could not provide.[1]

# 4
# A WORLD FORGETTING

The first half of human history—roughly five hundred thousand years—is a story not of triumphant progress but of agonizingly slow development punctuated by repeated collapse. It is the story of a species with extraordinary potential and almost no mechanism for preserving its gains.

## Two Outposts

During this long cultural twilight, two centers of culture managed to hold on. They were separated by thousands of miles, but between them they kept alive a faint thread of continuity stretching back to the original Andonite achievements.

In the west, the Foxhall peoples of England succeeded in retaining much of the Andonic culture. They preserved their knowledge of flintworking and transmitted it to their descendants, the ancient ancestors of the Eskimos. Though their remains were the last to be discovered in England, these Andonites were really the first human beings to live in those regions. At that time a land bridge still connected France with England, and since most of the early Andon descendants had settled along rivers and seashores, their sites now lie beneath the waters of the English Channel and the North Sea. Only three or four remain above water on the English coast—silent remnants of humanity's earliest European presence.

They were followed in Europe by a somewhat superior and prolific people whose descendants spread over the entire continent, from the ice in the north to the Alps and Mediterranean in the south. These are the tribes known as the Heidelberg race.

The other surviving center lay far to the east, in the foothills of the northwestern Indian highlands, among the tribes of a man named Badonan—a great-great-grandson of Andon himself. These Badonite peoples hold a unique distinction: they were the only descendants of Andon who never practiced human sacrifice. In a world where the killing of humans as a religious offering would become nearly universal, the Badonites refused. That refusal, maintained across hundreds of generations, speaks to something stubbornly admirable in this particular branch of the human family.

The highland Badonites occupied an extensive plateau surrounded by forests, traversed by streams, and abounding in game. Like some of their cousins in Tibet, they lived in crude stone huts, hillside grottoes, and semi-underground passages. While the tribes of the north grew more and more to fear the advancing ice, those living near Mesopotamia developed a different dread. They watched the Mesopotamian peninsula gradually sinking into the ocean. Though it emerged several times, the traditions of these primitive peoples grew up around the dangers of the sea and the fear of periodic engulfment. This fear, together with their experience of river floods, explains why they sought the highlands as a safe place to live. The geography of fear shaped settlement patterns that would persist for millennia.

## The Neanderthals

Around 850,000 years ago, the superior Badonan tribes launched a campaign of extermination against their inferior and more animalistic neighbors. In less than a thousand years, most of the borderland animal groups had been either destroyed or driven back into the southern forests. This violent purge brought about a slight improvement in the hill tribes of that age. And from the mixed descendants of this improved Badonite stock, an apparently new people emerged onto the stage of action: the Neanderthal race.

The Neanderthals were excellent fighters, and they traveled extensively. They gradually spread from the highland centers in northwest India to France on the west, China on the east, and even down into northern Africa. They dominated the world for almost half a million years—until the times of the migration of the evolutionary races of color.

By 800,000 years ago, game was abundant across Europe: many species of deer, elephants, hippopotamuses, plentiful cattle, and horses and wolves everywhere. The Neanderthals were great hunters, and the tribes in France were the first to adopt the practice of giving the most successful hunters the choice of women for wives—a social innovation that directly rewarded hunting skill and tied reproductive success to practical competence.

The reindeer was especially useful, serving as food, clothing, and raw material for tools, since the Neanderthals made various uses of its horns and bones. They had little culture in the broader sense, but they greatly improved the work in flint until it almost reached the levels of Andon's own era. Large flints attached to wooden handles came back into use, serving as axes and picks. The fact that flint tools had to be *re*-improved to levels achieved hundreds of thousands of years earlier tells you everything about the fragility of progress in this period.

## The Glaciers

The ice shaped everything. By 750,000 years ago, the fourth ice sheet was well on its way south, making its most extensive invasion of Europe. With their improved implements, the Neanderthals made holes in the ice covering the northern rivers and speared the fish that came up to these vents—a clever adaptation to a landscape that was becoming increasingly hostile. But they could not hold their ground. The tribes retreated steadily before the advancing cold.

The Siberian glacier made its southernmost march during this period, compelling early humans to move back toward the lands of their origin. But by now, the human species had differentiated enough that the danger of mingling with nonprogressive simian relatives was greatly lessened. Humanity had moved far enough from its animal cousins, both geographically and biologically, that backsliding into the simian world was no longer a serious threat.

By 700,000 years ago, the fourth glacier—the greatest of all in Europe—was in recession. Humans and animals returned north. The climate was cool and moist, and primitive peoples again thrived in Europe and western Asia. But then, around 550,000 years ago, the advancing glacier pushed humans and animals south once more. This time, however, there was plenty of room in the wide belt of land stretching northeast into Asia, between the ice sheet and the greatly expanded Black Sea extension of the Mediterranean.

## The Religion of Fear

The Neanderthals really had no religion beyond a shameful superstition. They were deathly afraid of clouds, and especially of mists and fogs. A primitive religion of fear gradually developed around natural forces: thunder, lightning, wind, and darkness. As their food supply became more reliable, the old animal worship declined, replaced by attempts to placate the invisible forces behind these terrifying natural phenomena. This escalation of superstition eventually culminated in human sacrifice.

The logic, if it can be called that, was grimly straightforward. The Neanderthals could hardly be called sun worshipers—they lived in fear of the dark and had a mortal dread of nightfall. As long as the moon shone even a little, they managed. But in the dark of the moon, they grew panicky and began sacrificing their best specimens of manhood and womanhood in an effort to induce the moon to shine again. The sun, they had learned, would reliably return each morning. But the moon, they conjectured, only returned because they sacrificed their fellow tribesmen. The terrible internal logic of this belief—that the disappearance of the moon *proved* the need for sacrifice, and its reappearance *proved* the sacrifice had worked—made it nearly impossible to break. As the race advanced, the object and purpose of sacrifice progressively changed, but the offering of human life as a religious act persisted for an appallingly long time.

## The Darkest Age

The times of the fourth and fifth glaciers witnessed the further spread of the crude Neanderthal culture, but almost no real advancement. For nearly a quarter of a million years, these primitive peoples drifted on—hunting and fighting, by spells improving in certain directions, but on the whole steadily retrogressing compared with their superior Andonic ancestors. During these spiritually dark ages, the culture of superstitious humanity reached its lowest levels.

It is worth pausing to absorb the scale of this stagnation. A quarter of a million years is not a figure that fits comfortably in the human imagination. It is roughly a thousand times longer than the entire span from the Roman Empire to the present day. And for that entire immense stretch of time, the human project appeared to be failing. Progress was so minimal that it truly seemed as though the attempt to produce a new and modified type of intelligent life on this world was about to fail altogether.

The Andonites had proven that human beings could survive. The Neanderthals were proving that survival alone was not enough. Something more was needed—some new infusion of capacity, some break in the long, grinding cycle of stagnation and decline.

Half a million years into the human experiment, that break came from the most unexpected of sources: a single family, in the highlands where the story had begun.

## The Sangik Family

Five hundred thousand years ago, in the same northwestern Indian highlands where the Badonites had maintained their culture for hundreds of millennia, a brutal war broke out. For more than a hundred years the fighting raged. When it was finished, only about one hundred families were left. But these survivors were the most intelligent and desirable of all the then-living descendants of Andon and Fonta. The war had been a catastrophe, but it had also been a crucible.

Among these surviving highland Badonites, a new and strange occurrence took place. A man and woman living in the north-eastern part of the inhabited highland region began suddenly to produce a family of unusually intelligent children. This was the Sangik family, the ancestors of all six colored races.

The Sangik children numbered nineteen. They were not only more intelligent than their peers, but their skins manifested a unique tendency to turn various colors upon exposure to sunlight. Among the nineteen were five red, two orange, four yellow, two green, four blue, and two indigo. These colors became more pronounced as the children grew older, and when they later mated with their fellow tribesmen, all of their offspring tended toward the skin color of the Sangik parent. The trait was dominant and persistent. From one family, the entire spectrum of human racial diversity had appeared.

This was extraordinary by any standard. On an average evolutionary planet, the six evolutionary races of color appear one by one over long stretches of time. The red race evolves first and roams the world for ages before the next colored race makes its appearance. The simultaneous emergence of all six races in one family was most unusual—a departure from the typical pattern of human development even more striking than the earlier appearance of the Andonites themselves.

## The Great Dispersal

For almost one hundred thousand years after their appearance, the Sangik peoples spread out around the foothills of their highland home, mingling with each other despite the peculiar but natural antipathy that early manifested itself between the different races.

The primary Sangik races—the red, yellow, and blue—generally avoided the tropics. The red race moved northeast into Asia, closely followed by the yellow race, while the blue race moved northwest into Europe. The secondary races—the orange, green, and indigo—tended southward. India became the most cosmopolitan population center on the planet during this period, the mixture there including heavy concentrations of the green, orange, and indigo stocks.

The fifth glacier was advancing as the Sangik descendants began to multiply and seek new territory. Ice to the north, mountains to the east, sea to the south and west—the same constraints that had funneled the Andonites now directed the colored races along similar paths, though to very different destinations.

The age of a single human stock—one race, one language family, one set of cultural traditions—was over. In its place was a world of dramatic diversity: six distinct peoples with different physical characteristics, different temperaments, and different developmental trajectories, all descended from one family, itself descended from Andon and Fonta nearly half a million years before.

The long decline was over. The age of the colored races had begun.[1]

# 5

# THE PRIMARY
# COLORED RACES

Of the six colored races that emerged from the Sangik family, three were designated primary: the red, the yellow, and the blue. Each originated from four or five of the nineteen Sangik children, giving them a larger founding population than the secondary peoples. But the difference was more than numerical. The primary races demonstrated greater intellectual capacity, greater social adaptability, and greater staying power across the immense stretches of time that followed. Each would stamp an entire continent with its presence. Each would produce at least one leader whose spiritual insight reached toward monotheism. And each would persist long enough to shape the civilizations that came after them—though by very different paths and at very different costs.

## The Red Race

The red men were in many ways the most advanced of all the Sangik peoples—remarkable specimens of the human race, in many ways superior to Andon and Fonta themselves. They were a most intelligent group and the first of the Sangik children to develop a tribal civilization and government. They were always monogamous, a trait that distinguished them from several of the other colored races and contributed to more stable family structures. They early invented the bow and arrow, a technological achievement that gave them decisive advantages in both hunting and warfare.

The red race was the first of the Sangik peoples to migrate from the central Asian highlands, and they established themselves across eastern Asia with striking speed. The red man had reigned supreme in eastern Asia for almost one hundred thousand years before the yellow tribes arrived. For a time, they were the dominant human presence across the accessible regions of the continent.

But supremacy did not last. More than three hundred thousand years ago, the main body of the yellow race entered China from the south as coastwise migrants. Each millennium they penetrated farther inland, and growing population pressure drove them northward into the red man's hunting grounds. What followed was one of the longest conflicts in human history. For over two hundred thousand years these two races waged bitter and unremitting warfare. In the earlier struggles, the red men were generally successful, their raiding parties spreading havoc among the yellow settlements. But the yellow man was an apt pupil in the art of warfare, and he early manifested a marked ability to live peaceably with his compatriots. The Chinese were the first to learn that in union there is strength.

That single insight decided the outcome. The red tribes continued their internecine conflicts even as they fought the yellow race, dividing their strength at the worst possible moment. The yellow tribes maintained internal cohesion and presented a unified front. Slowly, inexorably, the red man was pushed north and east toward colder and less hospitable territory.

One hundred thousand years ago, the decimated tribes of the red race were fighting with their backs to the retreating ice of the last glacier. When the land passage to the west, over the Bering isthmus, became passable, these tribes were not slow in forsaking the inhospitable shores of the Asiatic continent. About eighty-five thousand years ago, the comparatively pure remnants of the red race went en masse across to North America, and shortly thereafter the Bering land isthmus sank, isolating them completely. No red man ever returned to Asia. But the long struggle left its genetic imprint upon the victorious yellow race. The northern Chinese peoples, together with the Andonite Siberians, assimilated much of the red stock and were in considerable measure benefited thereby.

When the red man crossed over into America, he brought along much of the teachings and traditions of his early origin. But in a short time after reaching the Americas, the red men began to lose sight of these teachings, and there occurred a great decline in intellectual and spiritual culture. Very soon these people again fell to fighting so fiercely among themselves that it appeared these tribal wars would result in the speedy extinction of this remnant of the comparatively pure red race.

Because of this great retrogression the red men seemed doomed when, about sixty-five thousand years ago, Onamonalonton appeared as their leader and spiritual deliverer. He brought temporary peace among the American red men and revived their worship of the "Great Spirit." Consider the scale of what this man accomplished. At a moment when tribe was annihilating tribe across two continents, one individual persuaded them to stop. He achieved something the red race had never known and would never know again: universal peace.

Onamonalonton lived to be ninety-six years of age and maintained his headquarters among the great redwood trees of California. Many of his later descendants have come down to modern times among the Blackfoot peoples. But as time passed, his teachings became hazy traditions. Internecine wars resumed, and never after the days of this great teacher did another leader succeed in bringing universal peace among them. Increasingly the more intelligent strains perished in these tribal struggles. Otherwise a great civilization would have been built upon the North American continent by these able and intelligent red men.

After crossing over to America from China, the northern red man never again came in contact with other world influences —except the Eskimo—until he was later discovered by the white man. About five thousand years ago, a chance meeting occurred between a red race tribe and a lone Eskimo group on the southeastern shores of Hudson Bay. These two tribes found it difficult to communicate with each other, but very soon they intermarried, with the result that these Eskimos were eventually absorbed by the more numerous red men. This represents the only contact of the North American red man with any other human stock down to about one thousand years ago, when the white man first chanced to land on the Atlantic coast.

The red and the yellow races are the only early human stocks that ever achieved a high degree of civilization apart from the influences of the Andites. The oldest Native American culture was the Onamonalonton center in California, but this had long since vanished by 35,000 B.C. In Mexico, Central America, and in the mountains of South America, the later and more enduring civilizations were founded by a race predominantly red but containing a considerable admixture of the yellow, orange, and blue.

Isolated from the rest of humanity for tens of thousands of years, the red race built civilizations from nothing but their own endowment. What they achieved alone on two continents, without the contributions that accelerated progress everywhere else, stands as a testament to what a single Sangik race could do.

## The Yellow Race

The primitive yellow tribes were the first to abandon the chase, establish settled communities, and develop a home life based on agriculture. Intellectually they were somewhat inferior to the red man, but socially and collectively they proved themselves superior to all of the Sangik peoples in the matter of fostering racial civilization. The transition from hunting to agriculture was among the most consequential shifts in human history, and the yellow race made it before anyone else. Surplus food, stable populations, complex social structures—all the prerequisites of advanced civilization followed from that single change.

Because they developed a fraternal spirit, the various tribes learning to live together in relative peace, they were able to drive the red race before them as they gradually expanded into Asia. While the red race repeatedly weakened itself through internal warfare, the yellow tribes maintained sufficient unity to present a formidable collective front. This social cohesion, more than individual brilliance or military prowess, proved to be their greatest strength.

They traveled far from early centers of culture and drifted into spiritual darkness over many millennia. But there occurred one brilliant age when Singlangton, about one hundred thousand years ago, assumed the leadership of these tribes and proclaimed the worship of the "One Truth." A hundred thousand years before Moses, before Buddha, before any figure in recorded religious history, this man looked past the spirits and ghosts that populated every primitive religion and proclaimed that behind all of it stood one reality. That idea—the One Truth—would thread through Chinese thought for a hundred millennia.

The survival of comparatively large numbers of the yellow race is due to their intertribal peacefulness. From the days of Singlangton to the times of modern China, the yellow race has been numbered among the more peaceful of the nations of Earth.

The success of the ancient yellow race rested on several factors working together. Genetically, unlike their blue cousins in Europe, both the red and yellow races had largely escaped mixture with less progressive human stocks. The northern Chinese were strengthened by absorption of red and Andonite strains. Socially, the yellow man early learned the value of internal peace, and that peaceableness contributed to population growth and the spread of their civilization across enormous territories. Spiritually, long adherence to the worship of the One Truth proclaimed by Singlangton kept them ahead of most other races. The stimulus of a progressive religion in which truth was enshrined as the supreme Deity proved provocative of research and fearless exploration of the laws of nature and the potentials of mankind. And geographically, China's mountain barriers to the west and the Pacific to the east created a relatively secure heartland. Only in the north was the way open to attack, and even that corridor was partially shielded after the red race's departure.

Twenty thousand years ago, the ancestors of the Chinese had built up a dozen strong centers of primitive culture and learning, especially along the Yellow River and the Yangtze. From 25,000 to 5,000 B.C., the highest mass civilization on Earth was in central and northern China. The yellow man was first to achieve a racial solidarity—the first to attain a large-scale cultural, social, and political civilization. The Chinese of 15,000 B.C. were aggressive militarists; they had not been weakened by an overreverence for the past, and numbering less than twelve million, they formed a compact body speaking a common language. During this age they built up a real nation, much more united and homogeneous than their later political unions.

The yellow race did progressively move forward in the realization of the arts of civilization, especially in agriculture. The hydraulic problems faced by the agriculturists in Shensi and Honan demanded group cooperation for their solution. Such irrigation and soil-conservation difficulties contributed in no small measure to the development of interdependence and the consequent promotion of peace among farming groups. Developments in writing, together with the establishment of schools, contributed to the dissemination of knowledge on a previously unequaled scale.

And so the ancient civilization of the yellow race has persisted down through the centuries. It is almost forty thousand years since the first important advances were made in

Chinese culture, and though there have been many retrogressions, the civilization of the sons of Han comes the nearest of all to presenting an unbroken picture of continual progression. Forty thousand years of continuous culture. No other race can claim that. While other civilizations rose and fell and were forgotten, the sons of Han endured—building, adapting, absorbing, persisting. Whatever else this account reveals about the yellow race, that single fact speaks for itself.

## The Blue Race

The blue men were a great people. They early invented the spear and subsequently worked out the rudiments of many of the arts of modern civilization. The blue man had the brain power of the red man associated with the soul and sentiment of the yellow man—a combination of intellectual capacity and emotional depth that gave them a unique blend of capabilities among the Sangik peoples.

The blue race established itself firmly in Europe, where it would persist for hundreds of thousands of years. The European researches and explorations of the Old Stone Age have largely to do with unearthing the tools, bones, and artcraft of these ancient blue men, for they persisted in Europe until recent times. While we speak of the blue man as pervading the European continent, there were scores of racial types. Even thirty-five thousand years ago, the European blue races were already a highly blended people carrying strains of both red and yellow, while on the Atlantic coastlands and in the regions of present-day Russia they had absorbed a considerable amount of Andonite blood, and to the south were in contact with the Saharan peoples.

The blue men were hunters, fishers, and food gatherers. They were expert boatbuilders, navigating rivers and coastal waters to expand their range. They made stone axes, cut down trees, and erected log huts, partly below ground and roofed with hides—structures adapted to the harsh northern European climate. The southern blue men generally lived in caves and grottoes.

These peoples were brave and farseeing. They maintained an efficient system of child culture. Both parents participated in these labors, and the services of the older children were fully utilized. Each child was carefully trained in the care of caves, in art, and in flint chipping. At an early age the women were well versed in the domestic arts and in crude agriculture, while the men were skilled hunters and courageous warriors. This systematic approach to child-rearing—both parents contributing, older children teaching younger ones, practical skills transmitted through hands-on training—helped preserve and advance their knowledge across generations in the absence of writing.

It was not uncommon during the rigors of winter for their sentinels standing on night guard at cave entrances to freeze to death. They had courage, but above all they were artists. The height of the blue man's art was about fifteen thousand years ago—the cave paintings, the carved tools, and the cultural remains that fill European museums today. When we speak of the Old Stone Age in Europe, we are speaking, whether we know it or not, of the blue race.

About fifteen thousand years ago, the Alpine forests were spreading extensively. The European hunters were being driven to the river valleys and to the seashores by the same climatic changes that were transforming landscapes across the world. As the rain winds shifted to the north, the great open grazing lands of Europe became covered by forests. These great and relatively sudden climatic modifications drove the races of Europe to change from open-space hunters to herders, and in some measure to fishers and tillers of the soil. The open hunting grounds that had sustained their traditional way of life for hundreds of millennia disappeared within a few generations, forcing adaptations that would reshape European culture permanently.

The ancient centers of blue race culture were located along all the rivers of Europe, but only the Somme now flows in the same channel which it followed during earlier times. Europe's rivers have shifted course over hundreds of thousands of years, but the blue race's presence along them left marks that outlasted the rivers themselves. From the Mediterranean coast to the northern reaches of the continent, they owned that land for ages beyond counting. What came after them—as later chapters will show—was built on what they left behind.[1]

# 6

# THE SECONDARY COLORED RACES

Three of the six Sangik races were designated secondary: the orange, the green, and the indigo. Each originated from only two of the nineteen Sangik children, compared to the four or five who founded each primary race. This numerical difference at the origin foreshadowed a broader pattern—the secondary races demonstrated less capacity for building advanced civilizations, less ability to sustain cultural progress across generations, and ultimately less durability as distinct peoples. Two of the three would vanish entirely. The third would endure, but in isolation.

Their stories are briefer and harsher than those of the primary colored races. But they are no less part of the human record.

## The Orange Race

The outstanding characteristic of the orange peoples was their peculiar urge to build—to build anything and everything, even to the piling up of vast mounds of stone just to see which tribe could build the largest mound. This was not construction driven by practical need or strategic calculation. It was something closer to compulsion, an impulse to shape the physical world that consumed enormous labor without producing lasting infrastructure. Yet it demonstrated, however inefficiently, a creative drive that separated even the least progressive humans from the animal world.

The orange race was not a progressive people, though they did benefit from early centers of learning that existed in those ancient times. They were the first of the colored races to follow the coastline southward toward Africa as the Mediterranean Sea withdrew to the west. But they never secured a favorable footing on the continent—unable to establish the kind of dominant position that might have ensured their survival.

Before the end came, the orange peoples lost much cultural and spiritual ground. But there was a genuine revival under Porshunta, the master mind of this unfortunate race, who ministered to them when their headquarters was at Armageddon some three hundred thousand years ago. Like Onagar before him and Onamonalonton after, Porshunta demonstrated that a single exceptional leader could lift an entire people—and that the death of such a leader could leave them with no one to carry the work forward.

The last great struggle between the orange and the green peoples occurred in the region of the lower Nile valley in Egypt. This long-drawn-out battle was waged for almost one hundred years, and at its close very few of the orange race were left alive. The shattered remnants were absorbed by the green and by the later-arriving indigo peoples. As a race, the orange man ceased to exist about one hundred thousand years ago— roughly four hundred thousand years after emerging from the

Sangik family. They were the first of the six colored peoples to disappear from the planet.

## The Green Race

The green race was one of the less able groups of primitive peoples, and they were greatly weakened by extensive migrations in different directions. Rather than maintaining the concentration of population that might have given them strength through numbers, they scattered—and scattering proved fatal.

Before their dispersion, these tribes experienced a great revival of culture under the leadership of Fantad, some three hundred and fifty thousand years ago. Fantad was the green race's one exceptional mind, the leader who proved, however briefly, that even a secondary people could rise. But like Porshunta's revival among the orange peoples, Fantad's achievement could not survive his death. Without him, the green race resumed its decline.

The green race split into three major divisions, each meeting a different fate. The northern tribes were subdued, enslaved, and absorbed by the yellow and blue races—the more capable primary peoples who dominated the regions into which the green had migrated. The eastern group amalgamated with the Indian peoples of those days, and remnants still persist among them. India, acting as a catch basin for migrating races, absorbed the eastern green peoples into its already complex racial mixture.

The southern nation entered Africa, where they destroyed their almost equally inferior orange cousins in the prolonged Nile valley conflict. In many ways both groups were evenly matched in this struggle, since each carried strains of the giant order—many of their leaders being eight and nine feet in height. These giant strains of the green race were mostly confined to this southern division. The presence of giants on both sides helps explain why the conflict lasted nearly a century: neither side could achieve a quick victory.

But victory over the orange race did not save the green. The remnants of the victorious green peoples were subsequently absorbed by the indigo race, the last of the colored peoples to develop and emigrate from the original Sangik center. The green race had destroyed one people and was in turn absorbed by another. Their victory in Egypt proved pyrrhic—they had won a war only to lose their existence.

## The Indigo Race

The indigo race was the last of the Sangik peoples to migrate from the highland home, and the last to establish a continental homeland. They journeyed to Africa, taking possession of the continent, and have ever since remained there except when they have been forcibly taken away, from age to age, as slaves.

The indigo race's migration into Africa brought them into contact with the remnants of the green and orange races. By the time the indigo peoples began their major southward movement through Palestine and along the coast, the green race had already largely destroyed the orange in Egypt but had been severely weakened by the prolonged conflict. When the physically strong indigo peoples overran Egypt, they wiped the green man out of existence by sheer force of numbers. These indigo tribes absorbed the remnants of the orange peoples and much of the stock of the green, and certain of the indigo tribes were considerably improved by this racial amalgamation.

And so Egypt was first dominated by the orange man, then by the green, followed by the indigo. Eventually, the blue men of Europe and mixed races of Arabia drove the indigo race out of Egypt and far south on the African continent—a displacement that concentrated the indigo peoples in sub-Saharan Africa, where they would remain the dominant racial element for hundreds of thousands of years.

Isolated in Africa, the indigo peoples—like the red man in the Americas—received little of the contact with other developments that might have accelerated their progress. Alone in Africa, the indigo race made little advancement until the days of Orvonon, when they experienced a great spiritual awakening. In the deep interior of prehistoric Africa, cut off from every other center of culture on Earth, Orvonon arrived at something approaching monotheism—proclaiming a "God of Gods" to a people who worshipped spirits and feared ghosts. While they later almost entirely forgot what Orvonon taught, they did not entirely lose the desire to worship the Unknown. They maintained a form of worship up to a few thousand years ago—a thread of spiritual awareness stretching across millennia, however frayed.

Yet notwithstanding their slower cultural development, these indigo peoples have exactly the same standing before the celestial powers as any other earthly race. Whatever differences existed between the races in cultural achievement, technological development, or social organization, no race stands above or below any other in spiritual worth or eternal potential. The differences between races are real but temporal—they affect success in material civilization but do not determine the value of a single human soul.

———

By the time the major Sangik migrations drew to a close, the racial map of the world had clarified. The orange and green races were gone. The red man held North America, the yellow man eastern Asia, the blue man Europe, and the indigo race had gravitated to Africa. India harbored a blend of secondary Sangik stocks. The purer Andonites survived in the extreme northern regions of Europe, Iceland, Greenland, and northeastern North America.

Of the six colored races that emerged from one family half a million years before, only four remained as distinct peoples. The secondary races had served their part in the human story: the orange and green by contributing their genetic heritage to the peoples that absorbed them, and the indigo by enduring in Africa across the long ages—the only secondary Sangik people to survive as a recognizable race into modern times.[1]

# 7
# THE PLANETARY PRINCE

Five hundred thousand years ago, as the Sangik peoples were beginning their great migrations across three continents, something unprecedented happened. Humanity received outside help.

There were almost one-half billion primitive human beings at the time, well scattered over Europe, Asia, and Africa. Into their midst arrived a Planetary Prince and a corps of one hundred assistants, establishing headquarters in Mesopotamia at approximately the center of world population. For almost three hundred thousand years, this mission would guide humanity's development. Then it would be destroyed from within.

## One Hundred Volunteers

The Prince's staff were not native to Earth. They were volunteers chosen from over 785,000 ascendant citizens—beings who had already lived mortal lives on other worlds, died, and progressed through the early stages of the afterlife. They chose to return to material existence on a primitive planet. The sacrifice involved was real: they would leave behind a more advanced form of life to inhabit physical bodies and work among people who could not begin to understand what they had given up.

The process of giving them bodies was itself remarkable. Fifty males and fifty females from among the finest of the posterity of Andon and Fonta were selected—not as staff members, but as donors. A portion of their life plasm was transferred to the material bodies constructed for the use of the one hundred. The entire transaction of repersonalization consumed exactly ten days, after which the volunteers awoke as threefold beings of the realm—neither fully human nor fully superhuman, but something in between.

Their immortality was conditional. It depended not on any inherent biological property but on access to a particular tree —the tree of life—whose fruit sustained them through what the records call the antidotal complements of the life currents of the system. So long as they had access to this tree, they could live indefinitely. This detail, which might seem incidental, would prove catastrophic when the rebellion came.


## Dalamatia

The headquarters city was named Dalamatia. It was a very simple but beautiful place, enclosed within a wall forty feet high and laid out in ten subdivisions, each centered on the mansion of one of the ten working councils. At the heart of the city stood the temple of the Father of all—small, only three stories high, but centermost. The administrative headquarters of the Prince surrounded this temple in twelve chambers. The buildings were brick—very little stone or wood. This was not a grand capital by later standards. It was a teaching center.

Near the city dwelt people of all colors and social strata, and from these nearby tribes the first students were recruited. The schools were crude, but they provided all that could be done for the men and women of that primitive age. The real work happened not in the classrooms but in what the students carried home.

## The Ten Councils

The one hundred were organized into ten autonomous councils of ten members each. Reading through what each council worked on tells you as much about the state of humanity at the time as it does about the mission itself.

The **council on food and material welfare** taught well digging, spring control, and irrigation—meaning that before their arrival, half a billion humans had no reliable water management. They taught improved methods of treating skins for clothing; weaving was later introduced by their students, not by the staff themselves. They taught food preservation by cooking, drying, and smoking. Preserved food thus became the earliest form of property. Before you can own anything, you need something that lasts.

The **board of animal domestication** selected and bred animals for burden-bearing, transportation, food, and eventually soil cultivation. Several species they tamed are now extinct; others persist as domestic animals to this day. The cow was so improved by careful breeding as to become a valuable source of food—butter and cheese became common articles of human diet. Men were taught to use oxen for burden bearing, but the horse was not domesticated until a later date. Carrier pigeons were first used in these days for sending messages. The gap between oxen and horses tells you something about the pace of progress even with direct guidance.

The **advisers on predatory animals** addressed a problem easy to forget from a modern vantage: the world was full of things that wanted to eat you. Humans needed to learn not just how to domesticate useful animals but how to protect themselves from the hostile remainder. Improved techniques and traps made great progress in animal subjugation.

The **faculty on knowledge** formulated the first alphabet— twenty-five characters—and introduced a writing system. For writing material, these early peoples used tree barks, clay tablets, stone slabs, parchment made from hammered hides, and a crude paperlike material made from wasps' nests. The Dalamatia library comprised more than two million separate records.The destruction of that library in the rebellion repre- sents one of the great losses in human history—an archive of three hundred millennia of accumulated teaching, gone.

The **commission on industry and trade** fostered commerce between the various peace groups and, from a central exchange, developed a system of credits—tokens accepted in lieu of actual objects of barter. The world did not improve upon these business methods for hundreds of thousands of years. The invention of credit, in other words, happened not in Mesopotamia five thousand years ago but in Dalamatia five hundred thousand years ago—and then was lost and had to be reinvented.

The **college of revealed religion** was slow in functioning, which is an honest and telling detail. Spiritual development is harder to accelerate than technical development. This council provided seven chants of worship, a daily praise-phrase, and eventually taught the people "the Father's prayer":

"Father of all, whose Son we honor, look down upon us with favor. Deliver us from the fear of all save you. Make us a pleasure to our divine teachers and forever put truth on our lips. Deliver us from violence and anger; give us respect for our elders and that which belongs to our neighbors. Give us this season green pastures and fruitful flocks to gladden our hearts. We pray for the hastening of the coming of the promised uplifter, and we would do your will on this world as others do on worlds beyond."

This prayer was composed half a million years ago. Read it again slowly. "Deliver us from the fear of all save you"—a people haunted by terrors asking to fear only one thing. "Give us respect for our elders and that which belongs to our neighbors"—a people prone to violence learning the concept of legitimate ownership. "We would do your will on this world as others do on worlds beyond"—a people who had been told, by beings who had actually come from those worlds, that the universe was populated and purposeful. The prayer is a window into both the aspirations and the limitations of the people who spoke it.

The **guardians of health and life** introduced sanitation and primitive hygiene, teaching that cooking—boiling and roasting—was a means of avoiding sickness, and demonstrating that this greatly reduced infant mortality and facilitated early weaning. Before the Prince's arrival, bathing had been an exclusively religious ceremonial practice. These guardians also introduced handshaking in substitution for saliva exchange or blood drinking as a seal of personal friendship—a social reform so successful that we still shake hands today.

The **council on art and science** improved industrial technique and elevated concepts of beauty. Pottery advanced, decorative arts improved, and the ideals of human beauty were greatly enhanced. Music made little progress until much later. These primitive men would not consent to experiment with steam power, notwithstanding the repeated urgings of their teachers. The staff tried to introduce steam technology half a million years ago, and humanity refused. Whether from fear, incomprehension, or sheer stubbornness, they would not do it. The industrial revolution would have to wait.

The **governors of tribal relations** worked to bring human society up to the level of statehood, fostering intertribal marriages, courtship after deliberation, and competitive games and contests to replace purely physical combat. Sports as a substitute for warfare—another innovation so deeply embedded in human culture that its origin has been forgotten.

The **supreme court of tribal coordination** served as the court of appeals for all other nine commissions and handled all matters not specifically assigned elsewhere.

## The Mission

The one great task of those ages was to lead humans from hunting to herding, with the hope that later they would evolve into peace-loving, home-abiding farmers. The method was deliberate and respectful. The staff continuously gathered the superior individuals of surrounding tribes, trained and inspired them, and sent them back as teachers and leaders of their own peoples.

The key principle: foreign emissaries were never sent to a race except upon the specific request of that people. Those who labored for the uplift of a given tribe were always natives of that tribe. The one hundred would not attempt to impose the habits and customs of even a superior race upon another group. The simple peoples of Earth brought their social customs to Dalamatia not to exchange them for new and better practices, but to have them uplifted by contact with a higher culture and by association with superior minds. The process was slow but very effectual.

The Dalamatia teachers sought to add conscious social selection to the purely natural selection of biological evolution. Their motive was progression by evolution and not revolution by revelation. This distinction matters. They were not trying to replace human culture with something alien. They were trying to accelerate what was already happening naturally—and they had the patience to do it over hundreds of thousands of years.

## The Law and the Life

A moral law was presented to the early races, known as "The Father's Way." It consisted of seven commands:

1 You shall not fear nor serve any God but the Father of all.

2 You shall not disobey the Father's Son, the world's ruler, nor show disrespect to his superhuman associates.

3 You shall not speak a lie when called before the judges of the people.

4 You shall not kill men, women, or children.

5 You shall not steal your neighbor's goods or cattle.

6 You shall not touch your friend's wife.

7 You shall not show disrespect to your parents or to the elders of the tribe.

This was the law of Dalamatia for almost three hundred thousand years. Many of the stones on which it was inscribed now lie beneath the waters off the shores of Mesopotamia and Persia. The resemblance to later codes—including the Ten Commandments—is not coincidental. Moses did not invent these principles. He inherited them, through channels he could not have traced, from a city that had been underwater for hundreds of millennia.

At the outbreak of the rebellion, Dalamatia had a resident population of almost six thousand students, with visitors and observers always numbering more than one thousand. The country around the city was quite well settled within a radius of one hundred miles.

Family life as we know it dates from these times. The Prince's staff lived together as fathers and mothers. They had no children of their own, but the fifty pattern homes of Dalamatia never sheltered less than five hundred adopted little ones assembled from the superior families of the Andonic and Sangik races; many of these children were orphans. The concept of the nuclear family living together in one residence of comparatively settled location was taught by example before it was taught by instruction.

The plan of teaching was essentially an industrial school—pupils learned by doing, worked their way through by the daily performance of useful tasks. The plan did not ignore thinking and feeling in the development of character, but it gave first place to manual training.

# The Catastrophe

For almost three hundred thousand years, this system worked. It was humanity's first sustained exposure to superior guidance. Agricultural techniques spread outward from the teaching centers. Animal domestication advanced. Social organization improved. The colored races—especially the blue men, who were particularly responsive—absorbed teachings that accelerated their development dramatically. As noted in the previous chapters, several exceptional leaders among the various races drew upon the accumulated wisdom introduced through the Prince's mission, preserving and transmitting higher concepts even as direct connection to the teaching centers weakened over time and distance.

Then the rebellion came.

It was not an external attack. It was an internal fracture—a cosmic insurrection led by Lucifer, the system sovereign, that eventually found willing support in the Planetary Prince, Caligastia. Sixty of the one hundred corporeal staff members, led by Nod, defected. The loyal forty, led by Van, maintained their posts, but the damage was irreparable. The carefully constructed system of education and uplift collapsed. Dalamatia itself would eventually sink beneath the sea. The descendants of the rebellious sixty—who became known as the Nodites—would forge their own path, carrying both the gifts of the Prince's teaching and the corruption of the rebellion into human bloodlines.

The full story of the rebellion, its causes, and its consequences deserves its own book. What matters here is the scope of what was lost. Three hundred thousand years of systematic teaching, a library of two million records, a functioning moral code, a network of trained native leaders spreading outward from Mesopotamia, and a city that had become the cultural center of the world—all of it shattered by a betrayal from within.

Events would eventually unfold that would necessitate yet another attempt to uplift the struggling races of planet Earth.[1]

# 8

## HUNGER, FEAR, AND FIRE

Between the fall of Dalamatia and the arrival of the next great intervention—a span of roughly 160,000 years—humanity was largely on its own. The Prince's mission had collapsed. The Nodites carried fragments of higher knowledge but were themselves fractured and declining. The colored races were scattered across three continents. And the long, grinding work of building civilization fell to ordinary human beings, working without systematic guidance, learning everything the hard way.

What they accomplished in that time is remarkable. Not because progress was fast—it wasn't—but because it happened at all. The forces that drove civilization forward were not noble aspirations. They were hunger, fear, vanity, and the reluctant discovery that cooperating with people you didn't particularly like was better than dying alone.

# Fire

The discovery of fire by Andon and Fonta has already been told in this account. But fire's significance extended far beyond warmth and safety. By a single bound, fire forever separated humans from animals. It was the basic human invention, or discovery, and everything that followed depended on it.

Fire was used more for light than heat in the beginning—it allowed ground-dwelling at night, since all animals feared it. It protected against cold and wild beasts and was employed as security against ghosts. But its deepest civilizing effect was subtler. Fire was humanity's first means of being altruistic without loss. You could give live coals to a neighbor without depriving yourself. In a world where sharing meant going without, fire was the first thing that could be given freely—and that small fact opened a door in the human mind that would never fully close.

The household fire, tended by the mother or eldest daughter, became the first educator. It required watchfulness and dependability—qualities that had to be learned and transmitted. The early home was not a building but a family gathered about the fire, the family hearth. Before there were walls, before there were villages, there was the circle of light, and the person responsible for keeping it burning.

Fire led to cooking, and cooking was a revolution in itself. It lessened the expenditure of vital energy necessary for digestion, leaving early humans some strength for social culture. It greatly reduced infant mortality and facilitated early weaning. The guardians of health among the Prince's staff would later formalize these insights, but humans had been stumbling toward them for hundreds of thousands of years before Dalamatia was built.

Fire opened the door to metalwork, and metalwork would eventually open the door to everything else—tools, weapons, construction, and the long chain of technological development that leads, through steam power and electricity, to the present day.

## The Dog and the Herd

The entire animal world was initially humanity's enemy. Humans had to learn first to protect themselves from beasts, then to eat them, and only much later to domesticate them and make them serve.

The first animal domesticated was the dog. It began when a certain dog followed a hunter around all day and actually went home with him. For ages dogs were used for food, hunting, transportation, and companionship. At first dogs only howled, but later they learned to bark. The dog's keen sense of smell led to the belief that it could see spirits, and the employment of watchdogs made it possible for whole clans to sleep at night. That detail is worth sitting with: before the dog, someone always had to stay awake. The domestication of a single species gave an entire community the gift of rest.

Animal domestication came about largely by accident. Peoples who hunted herds discovered that by surrounding them, they could keep control of the animals and kill them as needed. Corrals followed. Eventually certain species proved willing to submit to human presence and reproduce in captivity. Selective breeding began. The cow was so improved by careful breeding as to become a valuable source of food—butter and cheese became common articles of human diet. Men were taught to use oxen for burden bearing, though the horse would not be domesticated until a much later date.

The pastoral stage—living on the increase of one's flocks rather than hunting for each meal—provided a kind of relief from food slavery. Humans learned to live on the interest of their capital. This provided leisure, and leisure provided time for culture and progress. But the pastoral revolution had a dark side. In earlier times, men hunted and women gathered—a rough equality of contribution. When animal husbandry became the primary livelihood, women's work in gathering vegetable food was devalued. By the close of the pastoral era, women had been reduced to something close to property, consigned to labor and bear children much as herd animals were expected to labor and bring forth young. Association with animals suggested struggle and force. The pastoral age was militant and warlike.

Agriculture reversed this. The growing of plants exerted an ennobling influence on all races and more than quadrupled the land-man ratio of the world. Association with plants instilled patience, quiet, and peace. The agriculturist was a more peace-loving type than the herder. The yellow race was the first to make this transition fully, and it was no coincidence that they became the most peaceful of the Sangik peoples.

## The Market and the Token

Trade began in silence and at a distance. The first barter was conducted by armed traders who left their goods on neutral ground. A fetish was placed to stand guard over the deposits of goods, and the marketplaces were secure against theft—nothing would be removed except by barter or purchase. For ages, silent barter continued before people would meet unarmed on sacred marketplaces. These same market squares became the first places of sanctuary, and in some countries were later known as "cities of refuge." Any fugitive reaching the marketplace was safe and secure against attack. The market, in other words, was sacred ground before it was commercial ground.

Women held the first markets. They were the earliest traders, because they were the burden bearers—and because the pattern of their work, centered on settlement rather than ranging, made them the natural managers of exchange. The first weights were grains of wheat and other cereals. The first medium of exchange was a fish or a goat. Later the cow became a unit of barter.

The commission on industry and trade at Dalamatia formalized what humans had been groping toward for millennia, developing from a central exchange a system of credits— tokens accepted in lieu of actual objects of barter. The world did not improve upon these business methods for hundreds of thousands of years. The invention of credit was ancient beyond reckoning, and the fact that it had to be reinvented after Dalamatia's fall tells you how fragile progress was in those ages.

Modern writing originated in early trade records. The first literature of the human race was a trade-promotion document —a salt advertisement. Many early wars were fought over natural deposits of flint, salt, and metals. The first formal tribal treaties concerned the intertribalizing of salt deposits. Commerce, not philosophy, drove the development of literacy.

# Ghost Fear

One force above all others held early society together and gave it structure: the fear of ghosts.

The ghost dream was one of the earliest differences between animal and human types of mind. Animals do not visualize survival after death. But humans did—and the dread of departed spirits reached out beyond elemental individual needs and rose far above the struggle to maintain the group. Ghost fear introduced a new and astonishing factor into civilization. It brought to light amazing forms of fear that contributed to discipline in the loose social orders of early ages, binding them into more thoroughly controlled primitive groups.

The mechanism was grimly effective. The dead were believed to be jealous of the ways by which they had lived and died. Anyone who dared treat with careless disdain the rules of living that the deceased had honored when in the flesh would supposedly suffer dire punishment. This meant that custom became sacred—not because anyone understood why a practice worked, but because the dead were watching and the dead were vengeful. The mores were preserved from generation to generation not by rational argument but by supernatural terror.

This was, in a sense, a prison. Prior to the liberating instruction from teachers like those at Dalamatia, ancient humans were helpless victims of ritual and custom. Everything had to be done according to the folkways of the tribe, from awakening in the morning to falling asleep at night. There was nothing free, spontaneous, or original. There was no natural progress toward higher mental, moral, or social existence.

And yet ghost fear was also, paradoxically, a foundation. It securely laid the groundwork for powerful social influences of ethics and religion. The baseless fears of evolution were designed to be supplanted—by awe for higher realities, by revelation, and by reason. The prison of superstition would eventually become the scaffolding for genuine spiritual life. But the transition was agonizingly slow, and for most of human history, the scaffolding looked indistinguishable from the prison.

## What Humanity Built

By the time the next intervention arrived—approximately 38,000 years ago—the scattered races had accomplished more than anyone observing Dalamatia's fall might have predicted. They had domesticated fire, animals, and plants. They had invented writing, trade, and credit. They had formed governments, legal systems, and military organizations. They had built cities and established religions. They had developed art, medicine, and metallurgy.

The progress was uneven, marked by frequent setbacks, wars, and catastrophes. Civilization advanced not in a straight line but in agelong cycles of advance and regression, driven by fear more than hope, by necessity more than vision. But the overall trajectory was upward. The price of survival had been paid through submission to society's demands—and in paying that price, humanity had built something that could receive and benefit from whatever came next.[1]

# 9
## THE NODITES

The rebellion had shattered the Prince's original mission. Sixty of the one hundred corporeal staff members had followed Caligastia into defection, led by Nod—formerly the head of the commission on industry and trade. But the story of the sixty was far from over. Their choice would give rise to an entirely new race—the eighth to appear on Earth—and their descendants would shape civilizations across the ancient world for tens of thousands of years.

## The Cost of Rebellion

The sixty rebels discovered almost immediately what their choice had cost them. The life circuits that had sustained them for hundreds of thousands of years were gone. They were still superhuman in many respects—possessing knowledge, abilities, and physical characteristics far beyond ordinary humans—but they were now subject to aging and death like any mortal. The tree of life, which had maintained their immortality, was no longer accessible to them.

Daligastia, the Prince's associate-assistant who had joined the rebellion, understood the implications and ordered immediate resort to sexual reproduction. Without the life-sustaining systems, the original rebel staff members and their forty-four modified Andonite associates were doomed to eventual extinction by death. If anything was to survive of their kind, it would have to be through their children.

After the fall of Dalamatia, the disloyal staff migrated to the north and east. Their descendants became known as the Nodites, and their dwelling place as "the land of Nod." The presence of these extraordinary beings—stranded by rebellion and now mating with ordinary humans—gave rise to numerous traditional stories found across many cultures. Tales of gods coming down to mate with mortals, producing heroes and demigods, were not mere myths but distorted memories of actual events from the post-rebellion period. Ancient tradition preserves the echo: "The Nephilim were on Earth in those days," and the legends speak of "mighty men of old" and "men of renown." Though hardly sons of the gods, the staff and their early descendants were so regarded by the evolutionary mortals of those distant days. Even their stature came to be magnified by tradition.

## The Eighth Race

When the sixty rebel staff members and their forty-four modified Andonite associates engaged in sexual reproduction, their children proved extraordinarily advanced beyond both the Andonite and Sangik peoples in almost every way—in physical and intellectual qualities, and even in spiritual capacities. The mechanism behind this was biological. The powerful life-maintenance circuits that had operated in the bodies of the staff members before those circuits were severed had caused the chromosomes of the specialized pattern to reorganize in ways that produced enhanced human characteristics. The effect was comparable to what modern science would later discover with X-ray-induced mutations—the life circuits had altered the inheritance factors of the Andonite germ plasm, and those modifications passed to the next generation.

Together, the sixty rebel staff members and the forty-four modified Andonites who followed them—one hundred and four individuals carrying this enhanced genetic material—constituted the ancestry of the Nodites. They arose not through evolutionary processes but through the unique circumstances of superhuman beings cut off from their life-sustaining systems and compelled to reproduce—passing their extraordinary endowment to children who proved superior to the surrounding peoples.

The pure-line Nodites were a magnificent race in their early generations. They possessed unusual longevity, exceptional physical qualities, and intellectual capabilities far exceeding the evolutionary peoples around them. But they gradually mingled with the surrounding populations, and deterioration inevitably followed. Ten thousand years after the rebellion, they had lost ground to the point where their average length of life was little more than that of the evolutionary races.

This decline left traces in the historical record. When archaeologists excavate the clay-tablet records of later Sumerian descendants of the Nodites, they discover king lists running back for several thousand years. As these records trace further into the past, the reigns of individual rulers lengthen dramatically—from twenty-five or thirty years up to 150 years and more. This is not fiction. It reflects the genuine longevity of the early Nodite rulers, though some confusion exists due to different methods of time reckoning in ancient periods. The long-lived kings of the early Sumerian lists were real people whose lifespans have seemed mythological only because the biological basis for their longevity has been forgotten.

## The Tower of Babel

One hundred and sixty-two years after the rebellion, a tidal wave swept up over Dalamatia, and the planetary headquarters sank beneath the waters of the sea. The Nodites moved north and east, eventually founding a new city called Dilmun as their racial and cultural headquarters.

About fifty thousand years after the death of Nod, the Nodite leaders faced a crisis of racial identity. Their numbers had grown substantially, and they had intermarried extensively with surrounding Andonite and Sangik tribes. A descendant of Nod named Bablot proposed the construction of a pretentious temple of racial glorification at the center of their occupied territory—a monument to Nodite greatness that would include a tower unlike anything the world had ever seen. The new city was named after its architect and builder, eventually becoming known as Bablod and ultimately as Babel.

But the Nodites could not agree on what the monument meant. After four and a half years of work, the divisions erupted into open conflict. Three competing visions had emerged.

Nearly half the population wanted the tower as a monument to Nodite history and racial distinction—a great and imposing structure that would challenge the admiration of all future generations. The next largest faction envisioned it as the centerpiece of a cultural center, with Bablot becoming renowned for commerce, art, and manufacturing. The smallest group saw the tower as an opportunity for atonement—a chance to make amends for their ancestors' participation in the rebellion by dedicating the structure to the worship of the Father of all.

The religious faction was promptly voted down. The majority rejected the teaching that their ancestors had been guilty of rebellion and resented such implications. This is a revealing moment: the descendants of rebels refusing to acknowledge the rebellion. The guilt was real, but acknowledging it would have required dismantling the entire basis of Nodite identity and pride. It was easier to declare the whole subject a slander.

Unable to settle the dispute between the remaining two factions through debate, they resorted to violence. The religious group fled south, while the other two fought until they had nearly destroyed themselves. The great tower was never completed.

About twelve thousand years ago, a second attempt to erect the tower of Babel was made. By this time the mixed races of Andites—blending Nodite and Adamite ancestry—undertook to raise a new temple on the ruins of the first structure. But there was insufficient support for the enterprise, and it collapsed under its own pretentious weight. The region remained known as "the land of Babel" for millennia thereafter.

## The Four Centers

The dispersion following the tower conflict scattered the Nodites and drastically reduced the numbers of pure-line members. This internal war prevented them from establishing the great pre-Adamic civilization they might otherwise have created. From this time, Nodite culture declined for over one hundred and twenty thousand years until it received new impetus through Adamic infusion. Even so, the Nodites remained an exceptionally able people, and their mixed descendants would later contribute significantly to various civilizations.

Four major centers emerged.

The western, or Syrian, Nodites were the largest group—the remnants of the racial memorialists who journeyed northward and united with Andonite populations. They contributed substantially to the later-appearing Assyrian stock.

The eastern, or Elamite, Nodites were the culture and commerce advocates who migrated into Elam in large numbers, uniting with mixed Sangik tribes. The Elamites of thirty to forty thousand years ago had become largely Sangik in racial composition, though they maintained a civilization notably more advanced than surrounding peoples.

A smaller central group settled at the mouth of the Tigris and Euphrates rivers and maintained greater racial integrity than the other Nodite populations. They persisted for thousands of years and eventually provided the Nodite ancestry that would blend with the Adamites to produce the Sumerian peoples of historic times.

This last point deserves emphasis, because it solves a genuine archaeological puzzle. Investigators have never been able to trace the Sumerians back to any clear origin point. They appear suddenly on the stage of history in Mesopotamia with a highly advanced culture—temples, metalwork, agriculture, pottery, weaving, commercial law, civil codes, religious ceremonies, and a writing system. The mystery dissolves when you understand that Sumerian origins extend back two hundred thousand years to the submergence of Dalamatia. Without any trace of origin elsewhere in the world, these ancient tribes appeared on the horizon of civilization with everything they had because they had been accumulating it for millennia in a continuous cultural tradition stretching back to the Prince's city itself.

Archaeological excavations have uncovered Sumerian clay tablets describing a remarkable settlement on the Persian Gulf near the earlier city of Dilmun—an earthly paradise "where the Gods first blessed mankind with the example of civilized and cultured life." The Sumerians knew their own origins. They just didn't know how far back those origins actually went.

The fourth group arose before the Bablot conflict. These northernmost Nodites were descendants of those who had forsaken the traitorous leadership of Nod and his successors, instead following the loyal Van. Some early associates of Van had settled about the shores of a lake that still bears his name, and their traditions centered on this locality. Ararat became their sacred mountain, holding much the same meaning for these Vanite peoples that Sinai later held for the Hebrews. Ten thousand years ago, the Vanite ancestors of the Assyrians taught that their moral law of seven commandments had been given to Van by the Gods upon Mount Ararat—a tradition that would later interweave with other narratives in the region, including the flood stories that would eventually enter Hebrew scripture.

# Born from Rebellion

The Nodites were a unique phenomenon in human racial history—a people who arose not from evolutionary processes but from the mating of superhuman rebels with ordinary humans. For tens of thousands of years they maintained cultural and intellectual advantages over surrounding populations. Their city-planning, their writing systems preserved from Dalamatia, their organizational capabilities, their religious and philosophical concepts—all of these flowed into the civilizations that grew up around and after them.

But they were also a people marked by division from the beginning. Born from rebellion, they could never agree on what that rebellion meant. The tower of Babel was not destroyed by divine intervention, as later traditions would have it, but by the Nodites' own inability to reconcile their competing visions of themselves. The racial memorialists wanted glory, the culturalists wanted commerce, and the penitents wanted forgiveness—and none of them could tolerate the others' answer.

By the time the next superhuman intervention arrived—the event we will examine in the following chapters—the pure-line Nodites had largely disappeared through intermixture. But their genetic and cultural contributions had been thoroughly distributed across Mesopotamia, Persia, Syria, and beyond. Every subsequent civilization in these regions would carry some measure of Nodite heritage—the legacy of a hundred and four rebels who chose wrong, lost their immortality, and built a race from the wreckage.[1]

# 10

## THE VIOLET RACE

Nearly 38,000 years before the twentieth century, two beings arrived on the planet with a specific mission: to biologically uplift the human races. Their names have echoed through mythology and religion ever since, though the real story bears little resemblance to the garden tale most people know. It is a story of noble purpose, genuine love, a catastrophic error of judgment, and centuries of quiet work in diminished circumstances. Its consequences still ripple through humanity today.

## Material Sons

Adam and Eve were not the first humans on Earth—not by hundreds of thousands of years. They were Material Sons, members of an order of beings created specifically to serve as biological uplifters on evolutionary spheres. Before coming to this dark world, they had lived on the administrative capital of the local system of inhabited worlds, where for more than fifteen thousand years they had served as directors of the trial-

and-testing physical laboratories, specializing in the modification of living forms. They knew what they were being asked to do. They had trained for it longer than most civilizations last.

When the call went out for volunteers to come to Earth—a world complicated by rebellion and isolation—the entire senior corps of Material Sons and Daughters volunteered. After careful selection, Adam and Eve were chosen for what they knew would be one of the most difficult assignments in the local system. They left behind one hundred offspring—fifty sons and fifty daughters—who served as faithful stewards of universe trust.

## The Garden

An elaborate garden had been prepared for them on a long narrow peninsula—almost an island—projecting westward from the eastern shores of the Mediterranean Sea. This was the Garden of Eden: a masterpiece of natural beauty enhanced by decades of careful planning by Van and his faithful associate Amadon, the two heroes who had maintained civilization's thread through the dark centuries following the Caligastia rebellion.

At the center of the Garden stood the temple of the Universal Father, and nearby grew the tree of life—a plant whose fruit could sustain the enhanced longevity of the Material Sons. The Garden contained plants and animals collected from around the world, cultivated and arranged to serve as a center of education, culture, and biological improvement for the entire planet.

When Adam and Eve arrived, thousands gathered to welcome them. They were physically striking—a little more than eight feet in height, with bodies that gave off a shimmer of light, the origin of the traditional halo that later artists would paint around the heads of holy figures. Their descendants would be characterized by light hair—yellow, red, and brown—and fair complexions, which is why the offspring of Adam and Eve came to be called the violet race.

But their distinctiveness went far deeper than appearance. Both Adam and Eve possessed physical and spiritual vision far superior to ordinary humans. They could see various orders of celestial beings, including angels and even the fallen Prince Caligastia himself—beings invisible to evolutionary mortals. Their children would inherit modified versions of these capacities.

## The Plan

The mission was straightforward in concept and staggering in scope: establish a center of advanced culture, train teachers and leaders from the surrounding tribes, build up a large violet-race population, and then gradually introduce Adamic genetic inheritance into all the evolutionary races through systematic intermarriage. Over thousands of years, this would uplift humanity biologically, intellectually, and spiritually.

For almost seven years after Adam's arrival, the Melchizedek receivers who had managed planetary affairs remained on duty, watching and advising. When they finally departed, turning the administration over to Adam, the real work began.

Life in the Garden was centuries ahead of anything else on Earth. The educational system alone would have been revolutionary: children changed activities every thirty minutes, older ones every hour—learning by doing, with play and humor recognized as essential to development. The Adamites understood something many modern educators have had to rediscover: that learning must engage the whole person.

Religious worship focused on the Universal Father. Adam worked to discourage blood sacrifice and introduce the concept of prayer as genuine spiritual communion rather than empty ritual. The seventh day was devoted to worship and self-culture—the origin of the Sabbath tradition. Family life set a new standard. Children were valued and nurtured. Marriage was honored as a partnership. Adam taught explicitly that the woman, equally with the man, contributes those life factors which unite to form a new being—a radical concept in a world where women were generally regarded as property.

The Garden's government recognized both men and women in positions of authority. The educational and cultural institutions were open to surrounding peoples. Adam established over one hundred primitive manufacturing plants beyond the Garden walls and developed extensive trade relations with nearby tribes. Ambassadors went out to surrounding peoples. Leaders from various tribes were trained and sent home. The Edenic culture was spreading outward exactly as intended.

But it was working slowly.

## The Default

After more than one hundred years, Adam and Eve were discouraged. The world was not improving as quickly as they had hoped. The races still fought. Ignorance persisted. And they were isolated—cut off from the normal counsel and support that Material Sons on other worlds received.

In their discouragement, they became vulnerable.

Serapatatia was the leader of the western Syrian confederation of Nodite tribes—brilliant, sincere, and genuinely sympathetic to the Adamic mission. He proposed that if the Nodites could have a leader born with partial Adamic inheritance, it would create a powerful bridge between the Garden culture and the surrounding peoples. The plan seemed reasonable. It seemed like a shortcut that served the greater good.

Eve, worn down by decades of slow progress and burdened by isolation, consented to bear a child with Cano—the most brilliant mind and active leader of the nearby Nodite colony, a man described as the spiritual leader of his people. She convinced herself she was merely accelerating the inevitable mixing of the races. But it was default—a violation of divine trust. Not rebellion against God, not a conscious choosing of evil, but an error of judgment born from impatience and discouragement.

When Adam learned what Eve had done, he was devastated. But he loved his mate with a supermortal affection, and the thought of continuing without her was more than he could endure. In full knowledge of what he was doing, he deliberately committed the same transgression. He sought out Laotta, a brilliant Nodite woman who headed the western schools of the Garden, and with premeditation shared Eve's fate.

The consequences were immediate. Adam and Eve lost their immortal status. The enhanced vitality sustained by the fruit of the tree of life was gone. They became fully mortal.

Their children faced a terrible choice. Those who had reached the age of choice—twenty years—could either remain on Earth with their erring parents or become wards of the higher authorities. Two thirds chose to leave. The separation of parents and children, with no knowing when or whether they would meet again, was one of the most sorrowful scenes in Earth's history.

## Leaving Eden

The aftermath turned violent. Adam's followers, enraged by what had happened, destroyed the nearby Nodite settlement, killing every inhabitant—including Cano, the father of Eve's unborn child. A larger Nodite army assembled in response. Adam, having no taste for warfare, chose to leave Eden rather than fight.

A caravan of some twelve hundred loyal followers departed with Adam and Eve, journeying eastward to settle between the Tigris and Euphrates rivers. There they established the second garden, building a new center of culture from scratch—this time without the advantages of the carefully prepared first Eden. No ready-to-eat fruit from cultivated trees. Unprepared soil. Hostile surroundings. The curse of earning bread by the sweat of your face was not divine punishment but the natural consequence of losing access to a garden that had been decades in the making.

## The Second Garden

Adam and Eve, though diminished, were not defeated. They brought seeds and plants from Eden, herds of domesticated animals, and above all their knowledge and their commitment to continue in whatever reduced capacity remained.

Their family at the time of leaving the first Garden consisted of four generations numbering 1,647 pure-line descendants. In the second garden, they had additional children. The violet race continued to grow. And though the original plan of systematic racial uplift had been disrupted, intermarriage between Adamites and surrounding peoples began naturally, introducing superior Adamic inheritance into the evolutionary races.

Eve headed a commission of twelve on race improvement. Before Adam's death, this commission had selected 1,682 of the highest type of women on Earth, and these women were impregnated with Adamic life plasm. Their children—1,570 superior men and women—were born and raised among their mothers' peoples, spreading Adamic inheritance outward into the accessible world.

By 19,000 BCE, the Adamites had become a real nation numbering four and a half million, having already poured forth millions of their progeny into the surrounding peoples. Despite the default, despite losing their enhanced longevity, the violet race had not only survived but thrived.

## Death

Adam lived for 530 years. He died of what might be termed old age—his body simply wore out. Eve had died nineteen years earlier of a weakened heart. They were both buried in the center of the temple of divine service in the second garden.

They had not accomplished their original mission. The systematic uplift of the human races had been thrown into confusion. Earth lost millennia of potential progress. But even diminished by their own mistakes, Adam and Eve had contributed enormously. Superior genetic inheritance that raised the ceiling of human potential. Advanced culture that accelerated civilization by thousands of years. Concepts of government, law, education, and religion far ahead of their time. And perhaps most importantly, a demonstration that even noble beings can make tragic mistakes—and that those mistakes do not mean the end of usefulness or the end of hope.

The blood of Adam and Eve would continue to flow outward through their descendants, blending with Nodite and evolutionary stocks to produce a new mixed race—the Andites— who would become the most dynamic force in human history. That story belongs to the next chapter.[1]

# 11

## THE ANDITES

More than twenty-five thousand years ago, in the regions adjacent to Mesopotamia where Adam and Eve had established their second garden, a new kind of people began to emerge. They were not a pure race. They were a blend—the primary mixture of the pure-line violet race, the Nodites, and the best strains of the evolutionary peoples, particularly the blue, yellow, and green races. To be considered Andite, a person generally carried between one-eighth and one-sixth Adamic inheritance in their ancestry.

This mixed origin was precisely their strength. It was the best all-round human stock to appear on Earth since the days of the pure violet race. They were adventurous, possessed of roving dispositions, and the most skillful and sagacious militarists the world had yet produced. They contributed humor, art, adventure, music, and manufacture wherever they went.

The Andites were not white. They were pre-white. They were not Aryan. They were pre-Aryan. They were neither an Occidental nor an Oriental people. But their inheritance would eventually give the later white races that generalized homogeneity that has been called Caucasoid. The physical features we associate with specific modern populations—Nordic tallness and blondness, Alpine stockiness, Mediterranean dark complexions—all came later, from the mixing of Andite stock with different local populations in different regions. The Andites themselves were something prior to all of these.

## The Migrations

The Andite story is fundamentally a story of movement. For ten thousand years, from roughly 15,000 to 6,000 BC, they poured out of Mesopotamia and Central Asia in successive waves that reshaped every continent they reached. Earlier Adamite migrations had already been flowing northward through Turkestan and westward toward Europe since 25,000 BC. But the Andite migrations proper—carrying not just Adamic blood but the combined vigor of three racial streams—began around 15,000 BC and continued with increasing intensity.

What drove them outward was partly temperament and partly necessity. Population growth in Mesopotamia outpaced the land's capacity. Climatic shifts were already beginning to dry out the highland regions of Central Asia. And the Andites' own restlessness made them poor candidates for staying put. They were builders who kept moving on to build somewhere else.

The last three great waves left Mesopotamia between 8,000 and 6,000 BC. Sixty-five percent entered Europe. Ten percent moved into Iran and Turkestan. Another ten percent headed east toward Sinkiang and the lands beyond. Ten percent crossed Arabia into Egypt. The remaining five percent stayed along the coast of Mesopotamia, blending with the populations already there.

By 12,000 BC, three quarters of the world's Andite stock resided in northern and eastern Europe. By the time the last waves departed Mesopotamia around 6,000 BC, the Andites had established themselves on three continents.

## Turkestan

The broad region of Central Asia stretching from the Caspian Sea toward China—became a crucial staging ground. The migrating Adamites and Nodites who entered this region found conditions suited to their pastoral and agricultural economy. Here, the blending of these stocks with the local populations produced what the records describe as the highest type of Andite culture.

But the climate was turning against them. By 8,000 BC, slowly increasing aridity in the highland regions of Central Asia began to drive the Andites down to the river bottoms and out toward the seashores. Lakes shrank. Grasslands dried. The populations that had flourished in Turkestan were forced into the great dispersals that would carry their culture eastward into China, southward into India, and westward into Europe.

One lasting contribution emerged from this region: the Aryan mother tongue. The language that formed in Turkestan blended the Andonic dialect of the area with the language of the Adamsonites and later Andites, producing the ancestor of the Aryan linguistic family—the root that gave Western tongues all of that similarity later scholars would recognize and classify.

# Eastward

About fifteen thousand years ago, the Andites began traversing the pass of Ti Tao in considerable numbers, spreading out over the upper valley of the Yellow River among the Chinese settlements of Kansu. They brought with them advanced agricultural knowledge and organizational methods. But the yellow race was no blank canvas—they had occupied China for more than three hundred thousand years and had already built impressive foundations of their own. There were four factors for the eventual superiority of Chinese civilization: the infusion of Andite and red racial blood, the natural peaceableness of the yellow peoples which allowed population growth, a long spiritual adherence to the worship of One Truth as taught by the ancient teacher Singlangton, and the geographic isolation provided by mountain barriers and the Pacific Ocean. Chinese merchants eventually traveled routes through Turkestan all the way to Mesopotamia, and cities rose after 10,000 BC as the Andite contributions merged with indigenous achievement. Yet the pattern here was the reverse of what happened in Europe—in China, the vastly larger yellow population absorbed the Andites rather than the other way around.

Farther south, the penetration of India came in multiple waves. About 15,000 BC, increasing population pressure throughout Turkestan and Iran occasioned the first really extensive Andite movement toward India. For over fifteen hundred years, these early migrants filtered through the highlands and mixed with the native peoples of the subcontinent—a population that already included representatives of all six Sangik races plus Andonites. The blending of these Andite conquerors with the native stock produced the Dravidian peoples. A second and more dramatic penetration came much later—the Aryan invasion, lasting almost five hundred years in the middle of the third millennium before Christ. This later wave was more military in character and would reshape India's cultural landscape. The Aryans instituted the great social castes in an effort to perpetuate racial identity, and they brought with them concepts of deity preserved from the traditions of the second garden. But India's story carried a sobering counterpoint to China's: here too, the Andites were ultimately absorbed by the far larger indigenous population, and the cultural and genetic contributions they brought were gradually diluted across the subcontinent.

## The Andites in Europe

Before the Andites arrived, Europe belonged to the blue man. By thirty-five thousand years ago, the European blue races were already a blended people carrying strains of both red and yellow ancestry. In their prime, they were brave, honest, and resourceful. The southern Cro-Magnons lived in caves and grottoes; throughout the continent they were expert boat-builders, skilled hunters and fishers, and makers of stone axes and log huts. But above all, they were artists. The Adamic mixture had suddenly accelerated their creative imagination, and the height of the blue man's art was reached about fifteen thousand years ago, before southern peoples moved north from Africa through Spain. Each generation carefully trained its children in the care of the caves, in art, and in flint making.

The Andites entered Europe by two primary routes. Some came by way of the Aegean islands and up the Danube valley, but the majority of the earlier and purer strains migrated to north-western Europe by the northern route, crossing the grazing lands of the Volga and the Don. Seven major invasions occurred in all, the last arrivals coming on horseback in three great waves. The horse proved to be the decisive evolutionary factor in Andite dominance of the west. It gave the dispersing Andites a hitherto nonexistent advantage of mobility, enabling the last groups of cavalrymen to progress quickly around the Caspian Sea and overrun all of Europe. Earlier waves had moved so slowly that they tended to disintegrate at any great distance from Mesopotamia, but these later mounted groups reached Europe as coherent peoples, still retaining some measure of higher culture.

Denmark became the military headquarters of the northern Andites for three thousand years, and from this base successive waves of conquest went forth, growing decreasingly Andite and increasingly white as the passing centuries witnessed the final blending of conquerors and conquered. The Cro-Magnons bitterly resisted the southward-moving Andites, and in the valley of the Somme they contested them for over five hundred years. The victorious commander who finally prevailed in those battles was Thor, who was later revered as a god by the northern peoples. By methods that combined military force, commercial penetration, population pressure along the rivers, and continued intermarriage with superior strains—coupled with the ruthless elimination of those deemed inferior—the Andites absorbed the blue man. By 5,000 BC the evolving white races were dominant throughout all of northern Europe, including northern Germany, northern France, and the British Isles.

The Cro-Magnon blue man constituted the biological founda-tion for the modern European races, but they survived only as absorbed by the later and virile conquerors of their homelands. The blue strain contributed much to the makeup of the white peoples of Europe, but as an independent culture it came to a swift end once the Mesopotamian horsemen appeared. In the north, the Andites obliterated the blue men through warfare and marriage, but in the south they survived in greater numbers. The Basques and the Berbers represent two branches of this ancient race that persisted into later times.

Central Europe held its own quiet chapter. The Danubian Andonites—farmers and herders who had entered Europe through the Balkan peninsula and moved slowly northward by way of the Danube valley—made pottery, tilled the land, and preferred to live in river valleys. Their most northerly settlement reached as far as Liège in Belgium. The ancient Hittites stemmed directly from this Andonite stock, with their characteristic pale skins and broad heads. Through the influence of Cretan missionaries, these Danubians became mother worshipers and practiced cremation. They were never entirely displaced by the Andites, and their broad-headed descendants persisted as a wedge of mountain peoples between the Nordic north and the Mediterranean south.

Toward the close of the Andite migrations, the racial blends in Europe became generalized into three broad groupings. The northern white race—later called Nordic—consisted primarily of blue man plus Andite, with considerable Andonite blood and smaller amounts of red and yellow Sangik. The typical early Nordic was long-headed, tall, and blond, though this race became thoroughly mixed long ago with all branches of the white peoples. The central white race—sometimes called Alpine—was predominantly Andonite, with strains of blue, yellow, and Andite. These people were broad-headed, swarthy, and stocky, driven like a wedge between the northern and southern groups with their broad base resting in Asia. The southern white race—the Mediterranean—was a blend of Andite and blue man with a smaller Andonite strain, further absorbing considerable secondary Sangik blood through the Saharans. In general, its members were short, long-headed, and brunet.

Yet rigid classification is misleading—there had been altogether too much blending to permit neat racial groupings, and no European population remained pure. These were tendencies, not boundaries. Meanwhile, the Andite legacy extended beyond the northern forests. About 12,000 BC, a brilliant tribe of Andites migrated to Crete—the first island settled by such a superior group—where they became highly skilled in textiles, metals, pottery, plumbing, and stone construction. On the African continent, Egypt became the successor of Mesopotamia as the headquarters of the most advanced group on the planet, and there the Andite genius Imhotep erected the first and most exquisite of the stone pyramids while serving as prime minister.

## The Sumerians

Back in Mesopotamia, the last identifiable Andite civilization was that of the Sumerians. They were the last of the Andites— a people who maintained a higher concentration of Adamic inheritance than the surrounding populations even as the broader Andite stock was being absorbed into the general human population.

The cities of Ur and Erech, Susa and Kish, Lagash and Akkad rose along the rivers of Mesopotamia, built on foundations that Andite culture had laid over millennia. But by the time of Hammurabi, the Mesopotamian Andites had passed from the pages of history. The racial picture had changed permanently. What had once been identifiable Andite populations had been absorbed through intermarriage into the much larger surrounding peoples.

## The Disappearance

By approximately 2,000 BC, the Andites as a distinct people had ceased to exist. But their disappearance was not failure. Their gift to humanity was never meant to remain separate. In every region they reached, they improved the genetic and cultural heritage of existing populations, raising intelligence levels, extending lifespans, improving physical health, and transmitting the accumulated knowledge of millennia.

The world they left behind was a world they had made. The cities, the trade networks, the agricultural systems, the languages, the organizational methods—all bore the stamp of Andite contribution, blended now with the contributions of every other race they had encountered. The Andites were the last major chapter in the long story of racial blending that began with Andon and Fonta and continued through the Sangik peoples, the Nodites, and the violet race.

That blending is not finished. It may never be.[1]

# EPILOGUE

Nearly one million years separates us from Andon and Fonta. In that span, every chapter of this book has unfolded—the long isolation of the early clans, the sudden emergence of six colored races from a single family, the slow building of tribal life into something that could be called civilization, the arrival and catastrophic failure of super-human guidance, the rise of the Nodites from the wreckage, the brief and radiant mission of Adam and Eve in the Garden, and the centuries-long dispersal of the Andites across three continents until they vanished into the peoples they had transformed.

It is a story of repeated beginnings. Every advance was followed by loss. The Prince's mission lasted three hundred thousand years before betrayal shattered it. The Garden experiment ended in default within a single generation. The Andites carried the combined inheritance of every prior uplift, and even they disappeared—not through destruction but through absorption into the larger human family. The pattern is consistent: the gift is given, the gift is partially lost, and what remains is absorbed into the broader stream of the race.

Yet something always survived. The moral code of Dalamatia echoed through cultures that had no memory of its origin. The biological contributions of the violet race persisted in populations that never knew the Garden existed. The Andite genius for organization, agriculture, and language shaped civilizations whose founders could not have named the source. The losses were real, but so was the persistence. Every generation inherited more than it knew.

What emerges from this account is not a story of human failure but of human resilience operating within a framework larger than any single race or epoch could perceive. The nine races were not accidents. The colored peoples were not random variations but distinct endowments, each carrying capacities the others lacked. The blending that followed—painful, violent, incomplete—was not a corruption of the original design but its fulfillment. Diversity was the method. Unity was the goal. The process is not finished.

The modern world inherits all of it. Every living person carries genetic threads that trace back through the Andites and Adamites, through the Nodites and Sangik peoples, through the long Andonic line, all the way to two children who fled their animal relatives and walked north into an unknown world because something in them recognized they were different. That recognition—the first stirring of genuine will, of moral awareness, of the capacity to choose beyond instinct— remains the defining characteristic of the species.

We are, all of us, the product of a million years of blending. The races described in these pages no longer exist as separate peoples. They exist as layers within every population on Earth, visible in the range of human temperament, capacity, and appearance but no longer separable into distinct streams. The process that began when the first Sangik children scattered from their family in the highlands of ancient India has reached a stage their parents could not have imagined. The world is becoming one people. It has been becoming one people for a very long time.

This book has told the story of how that process began. The rest of the story belongs to everyone who is living it.

# FROM THE AUTHOR

Thank you for reading. This book is the culmination of twenty years of seeking, study, and reflection.

If you're willing to share your thoughts, reader reviews make a meaningful difference for independent authors. Thank you so much.

# APPENDIX

The information in this book is drawn from *The Urantia Book*, a 2,097 page book first published in 1955 that claims to be a revelation presented by celestial beings to clarify and expand human understanding of cosmic reality and our place within it. This book about angels exclusively cites the 1955 edition which is in the public domain.

You may have never heard of it. Or you may have heard of it and dismissed it. That's fine. What matters is whether the information resonates as true, whether it elevates your understanding, whether it helps you live with greater purpose and confidence.

*The Urantia Book* has its critics and its devoted students. It's been called everything from the most important spiritual text of the modern era to elaborate fiction. I'm not asking you to accept it blindly. I'm asking you to read it and *then* decide if you think it is true. I do, and I have read it countless times.

The source is less important than the truth it contains. And if you want to explore further, *The Urantia Book* is available online and in print.

## About The Source Material

*The Urantia Book* is a comprehensive revelatory tome covering a wide variety of subjects including cosmology, philosophy, history and spirituality. It describes the nature of reality from the perspective of celestial beings and provides detailed information about the structure of the universe, the nature of God, the purpose of human existence, and the journey of the soul after death.

The book is organized into 196 papers grouped into four parts:

Part I: The Central and Superuniverses

Part II: The Local Universe

Part III: The History of Urantia (Earth)

Part IV: The Life and Teachings of Jesus

*The Nine Races* draws primarily from Part III: The History of Urantia (Earth). The following references are organized by chapter to help readers locate the source material corresponding to specific content in this book.

# NOTES

## 1. BEFORE THERE WERE RACES

1. Paper 62, Sections 1-5: The Dawn Races of Early Man — The Early Lemur Types, The Dawn Mammals, The Mid-Mammals, The Primates, The First Human Beings

## 2. THE FIRST HUMANS

1. Paper 62, Section 5: The Dawn Races of Early Man, The First Human Beings; Paper 63, Sections 1-4: The First Human Family — Andon and Fonta, The Flight of the Twins, Andon's Family, The Andonic Clans

## 3. THE PEOPLE OF THE DAWN

1. Paper 63, Sections 4-6: The First Human Family — The Andonic Clans, Dispersion of the Andonites, Onagar—The First Truth Teacher; Paper 64, Sections 1-2: The Evolutionary Races of Color — The Andonic Aborigines, The Foxhall Peoples

## 4. A WORLD FORGETTING

1. Paper 64, Section 1: The Evolutionary Races of Color, The Andonic Aborigines; Paper 64, Section 2: The Evolutionary Races of Color, The Foxhall Peoples; Paper 64, Section 3: The Evolutionary Races of Color, The Badonan Tribes; Paper 64, Section 4: The Evolutionary Races of Color, The Neanderthal Races; Paper 64, Section 5: The Evolutionary Races of Color, Origin of the Colored Races; Paper 64, Section 7: The Evolutionary Races of Color, Dispersion of the Colored Races

## 5. THE PRIMARY COLORED RACES

1. Paper 64, Section 6: The Evolutionary Races of Color, The Six Sangik Races of Urantia; Paper 64, Section 7: The Evolutionary Races of Color, Dispersion of the Colored Races; Paper 79, Section 5: Andite Expansion in the Orient, Red Man and Yellow Man; Paper 79, Sections 6-8: Andite Expan-

sion in the Orient, Dawn of Chinese Civilization, The Andites Enter China, Later Chinese Civilization; Paper 80, Section 3: Andite Expansion in the Occident, The Cro-Magnoid Blue Man

# 6. THE SECONDARY COLORED RACES

1. Paper 64, Section 6: The Evolutionary Races of Color, The Six Sangik Races of Urantia; Paper 64, Section 7: The Evolutionary Races of Color, Dispersion of the Colored Races

# 7. THE PLANETARY PRINCE

1. Paper 66, Sections 0-7: The Planetary Prince of Urantia; Paper 67, Sections 1-4: The Planetary Rebellion

# 8. HUNGER, FEAR, AND FIRE

1. Paper 68, Sections 1-3: The Dawn of Civilization, Protective Association, Socialization of Society; Paper 69, Sections 1-8: Primitive Human Institutions, The Utilization of Animals, Fire in Relation to Civilization, The Origin of Trade, The Beginnings of Capital; Paper 70, Section 1: The Evolution of Human Government, The Genesis of War

# 9. THE NODITES

1. Paper 67, Section 4: The Planetary Rebellion, The Caligastia One Hundred After Rebellion; Paper 67, Section 5: The Planetary Rebellion, Immediate Effects of Rebellion; Paper 77, Section 2: The Midway Creatures, The Nodite Race; Paper 77, Section 3: The Midway Creatures, The Tower of Babel; Paper 77, Section 4: The Midway Creatures, Nodite Centers of Civilization

# 10. THE VIOLET RACE

1. Paper 73, Sections 1-7: The Garden of Eden; Paper 74, Sections 0-7: Adam and Eve; Paper 75, Sections 0-8: The Default of Adam and Eve; Paper 76, Sections 1-5: The Second Garden

## 11. THE ANDITES

1. Paper 78, Sections 0–8: The Violet Race After the Days of Adam; Paper 79, Sections 1–7: Andite Expansion in the Orient; Paper 80, Sections 1–9: Andite Expansion in the Occident

# ABOUT THE AUTHOR

Michael Vincent spent years searching for answers that religion couldn't provide. Then he discovered *The Urantia Book* —a dense revelation that answered his questions with a coherence he'd never encountered. His work translates this complex material into books anyone can absorb.

*The Nine Races* is part of that project. Other books cover angels, cosmic history, Jesus, philosophy, and the structure of the universe itself.

michaelvincentauthor.com

# ALSO BY MICHAEL VINCENT

*Before Humans: The Drama of World-Making*

*The Missing Years: The Real Story of Jesus Beyond the Gospels* (The *Universe Maker from Nazareth* series, Book One)

*Where We Go When We Die: Life After Death Across the Universe*

*Fusion with God: The Path to Immortality*

*The Angelic Orders: Cosmic Servants of the Infinite*

Upcoming Books:

*The Public Ministry: The Real Story of Jesus Beyond the Gospels* (The *Universe Maker from Nazareth* series, Book Two)

*The Final Week: The Real Story of Jesus Beyond the Gospels* (The *Universe Maker from Nazareth* series, Book Three)

*Marcus Aurelius, Rodan of Alexandria, and Jesus of Nazareth: A Philosopher's Journey*